the Big Book of

SERVICE PROJECTS

Gospel Light
God's Word for a Kid's World!

HOW TO MAKE CLEAN COPIES FROM THIS BOOK

You may make copies of portions of this book with a clean conscience if

- you (or someone in your organization) are the original purchaser;
- you are using the copies you make for a noncommercial purpose (such as teaching or promoting your ministry) within your church or organization;
- you follow the instructions provided in this book.

However, it is ILLEGAL for you to make copies if

- you are using the material to promote, advertise or sell a product or service other than for ministry fund-raising;
- you are using the material in or on a product for sale; or
- you or your organization are not the original purchaser of this book.

By following these guidelines you help us keep our products affordable.

Thank you,

Gospel Light

EDITORIAL STAFF

Publisher, William T. Greig • **Senior Consulting Publisher,** Dr. Elmer L. Towns • **Publisher, Research, Planning and Development,** Billie Baptiste • **Managing Editor,** Lynnette Pennings, M.A. • **Senior Consulting Editor,** Wesley Haystead, M.S.Ed. • **Senior Editor, Biblical and Theological Issues,** Bayard Taylor, M.Div. • **Senior Advisor, Biblical and Theological Issues,** Dr. Gary S. Greig • **Editor,** Deborah Barber • **Editorial Team,** Amanda Abbas, Sheryl Haystead, Karen McGraw, Jay Bea Summerfield • **Contributing Editors,** Bonnie Aldrich, Anne Clay, Mary Gross, Janis Halverson, Linda Mattia, Mary Musgrave • **Designer,** Christina Renée Sharp

Contents

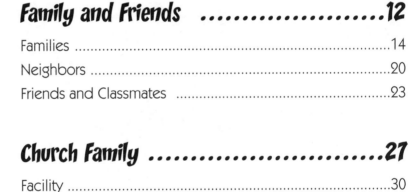

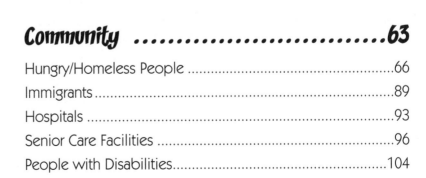

Missions and Outreach 105

Appendixes 137

Clip Art 151

Index 175

Articles

Why We Need to Serve

Teaching children to know and love God and then to show God's love to others is a noble goal—one of the most noble goals in this life. We can introduce students to the biblical concepts of service by asking questions and telling stories of heroic people who have loved and served God in the past; but with our children growing up in a "what's in it for me?" society, how can we help them put their learning into practice? How can we help them care about and be willing to serve others in response to God's love for them? *The Big Book of Service Projects* can help!

The Big Book of Service Projects is filled with ideas designed to help your students show God's love to the people around them and around the world. Service projects are not only the best cure for "me-itis," but they are also the natural response to many lessons we already teach in children's ministry; they allow us to take our students beyond simply hearing, talking about or even planning ways to love and obey God. Service projects motivate students to action: loving and obeying God as they assist others!

Service projects can help students

- encourage each other to do what God's Word teaches,
- experience the joy of giving to others,
- accept responsibility to complete a task,
- learn to work together, and
- recognize that God's Word leads His people to action.

The elements of a solid Christian education include Bible content, Bible skills, Bible memory passages, the lives of great Christians, Church history and more. However, the focus of Christian education must always be clear: to lead students to love God with all they are, to know God through Jesus Christ and to love the people around them as they love themselves.

Your students may at first find it a challenge to speak up, step out and make a difference. But after using some of the ideas in this book, you'll find that your students are hooked on the joy of sharing God's love!

How to Use This Book

Decide when to use service projects.

Whether you are teaching Sunday School, a midweek program, an after-school or weekend club, a choir or some other small group, this book can help you find fresh, new ways to expand your ministry!

Each activity is designed so that the major part of it can be completed in a classroom setting, and most projects take only 20 to 30 minutes to complete (except as noted). Ideas for delivering finished project items and/or expanding projects are also included where appropriate. All of these ideas used along with the Older and Younger Student Options allow you to customize the project to fit the needs of your students and situation.

Choose the right projects.

Thoughtfully select projects based not only on the needs of your church and community but also on what you know about your students' interests and abilities. Service project ideas are divided into four categories: **Family and Friends, Church Family, Community** and **Missions and Outreach.** Kids will easily connect with activities in the first three of these categories, because they will actually see the results of their actions. However, for kids to gain greater understanding of God's love for the whole world, they need to move from caring about those they know to caring about those they don't know. By participating in missions and outreach projects, students gain an opportunity to grow into people eager to serve God—anywhere!

Prepare your students.

When you introduce the first project, use the Bible passages and questions on pages 138-139 ("Introducing Service Projects") to help students understand the value of serving others. Refer to these Scripture passages often while you work together on projects. Help students remember that what they are doing is more than an interesting activity; it is living out what God says to do—which, they will learn, is an exciting way to live!

Talk with your students about the people they will be serving. If you are going to take them to visit people who are from a different culture or age group, tell students what to expect, giving them guidelines about how you expect them to act.

Involve parents.

Some projects will require parental notice (to solicit donations of goods, to notify of times and places students will be participating in an activity, etc.). Use the "Sample Parent Letter" on page 141 and the "Medical and Liability Release Form" on page 142 to keep parents informed and involved. Parents are often glad to help with donations, chaperoning and the like. And genuine teaching takes place when your students see willing adults gladly serving God in practical ways! Parents who volunteer their time and efforts should be given a photocopy of the Bible passages and questions on pages 138-139 to help them reinforce the values of and reasons for service.

Use all your resources.

Your church is probably full of people who are involved in serving others (doctors and nurses, teachers, social workers, missionaries, people involved in prison ministries and rescue missions, etc.). Talk with those you know and enlist their support for your projects.

Explore the resources in this book. Use some of the ideas you find here and then consider how you might expand on those ideas to create new ministries.

Encourage your students to be alert to new or unique ways to serve others and to share these ways with your group.

Enlist the prayer support of others.

You'll be amazed at the number of ways you'll discover to serve others. Read, listen, consider and pray—then go for it!

Service Questions and Answers

How can I find people who really need help?

Your pastor and other church leaders are great resources for finding people in your community and church family who could use help. The benefit here is that the recipients of your project's help aren't strangers and their needs are clearly known.

Phone calls to the local Red Cross or other local service organizations will get you started in the community (see "Service Organizations" on p. 146 for more ideas). Mission organizations are often eager to give you ideas for ways to help, as well as ideas to encourage missionaries and the people they serve. Contact information for a variety of mission and service organizations is listed on pages 147-148.

How do I introduce a project to my students?

To introduce a new project, talk briefly about the biblical basis for what you are doing. Remind students that serving others is a way to show love and obedience to God (see "Introducing Service Projects" on pp. 138-139). Get students' attention and build enthusiasm by telling them about the people they will be serving and how the students will be helping them. If possible, show pictures or video footage of the organization in action or invite a speaker from the organization to visit your class and talk with students. Lead students in praying for the people who will receive their gifts and in thanking God for the opportunity to show His love to others.

How can students deliver projects they have completed?

- Students can give items to the church leader or contact person who works with the people for whom the gifts are intended.

- Outside of class time, you can deliver the items to the appropriate people or organizations. You may want to take photos of the recipients to inspire your students to serve others more.

- Invite students to go with you to deliver items. Two or more weeks before the project, send home parent letters with permission forms (see pp. 141 and 142). After you have parents' permission, take students with you to deliver items. Invite several parent volunteers to go with you, so there is at least one adult for every six to eight students. When visiting people who live in different environments, talk with students ahead of time about what to expect. After the visit, take time to talk with students about what they experienced.

How can I keep kids' excitement and sense of accomplishment flowing?

- Take pictures or video footage as students work on projects. Make a project memory book or a memory video using photos of students, pictures of and information about the people the project was for and any letters or thank-you notes from recipients.

- Have a party! Review the projects you have completed. Show video footage of each project, look at pictures and letters related to the projects and give awards or certificates to members of your group in honor of ways they contributed.

- Provide names and addresses of recipients (where appropriate) so that students can write letters and stay in contact with the people they served.

- If you visited a convalescent home, shelter or other institution, have students write notes to those in charge, thanking them for allowing your group to visit and learn about what they do.

How can I help students care about others?

As kids begin to realize that they are helping real people, not just some distant organization, their enthusiasm will grow.

- Give students opportunities to meet the people they are serving. Take students with you to deliver projects to shelters, convalescent homes and homes of shut-ins.

- Talk with students about the people you are serving.

- Show pictures and video footage of people far away.

- Give kids e-mail addresses of missionary kids or others they support.

- Model it! Kids who see adult examples of compassion learn compassion. When the students see you and other adults actively caring about others in the projects you do, when the students hear the things you say to others and hear your prayers, they will begin to imitate that behavior. They will also begin to catch the vision and the excitement the adults around them model. Learning by watching adults who are enthusiastic about serving God is the most powerful form of education you can provide!

Service Projects

Family and Friends

Things to Do on Your Own for Your Family and Friends

MATERIALS

- ○ Things You Can Do at Home page (p.13)
- ○ photocopier
- ○ paper
- ○ scissors
- ○ construction paper or card stock in a variety of colors
- ○ glue
- ○ large envelopes
- ○ markers

PREPARATION

Photocopy Things You Can Do at Home page, making one copy for each student.

PROCEDURE

1. **What are some ways you have helped people in your family or your neighborhood? Let's make reminders of different ways we can help others each day.**
   Distribute materials to students. Students cut Things You Can Do at Home pages into strips, one idea on each strip. Students then cut construction paper or card stock into slightly larger strips and glue idea strips onto the larger strips.

2. Give each student a large envelope. Students decorate envelopes and place strips they prepared inside the envelopes.
   Encourage students to take envelopes home and each day try one idea from the envelope.

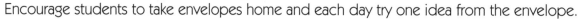

OPTION FOR YOUNGER STUDENTS

Each student chooses one of the ideas from Things You Can Do at Home page to cut out, glue to a sheet of construction paper and decorate. Encourage students to use the idea during the week.

OPTION FOR OLDER STUDENTS

Students brainstorm additional ideas of things they can do to help others at home and in their neighborhoods and write ideas on additional strips of paper.

Things You Can Do at Home

Try some of these ideas on your own!

Have a contest with yourself: See how many days in a row you can start your homework before your parents tell you to do it.

Say "Thank-you" to at least one person every day for a week.

Clean up trash you see on sidewalks in your neighborhood.

Pray for each person in your family before you go to sleep at night.

Invite a friend to go to church with you.

Bake some cookies for a neighbor.

Tell a friend five things you like about him or her.

Thank your parents for five things they have done for you.

Write a letter to a relative who lives in another place, and tell your relative about a Bible story or verse you have learned recently.

Invite a new kid at school to do something fun with you.

Breakfast in Bed

MATERIALS

- clear plastic cups
- permanent markers
- scissors
- wrapping paper or party napkins
- glue
- measuring cups
- oatmeal
- powdered milk
- sugar
- raisins
- resealable plastic bags
- large self-adhesive labels
- optional—fruit.

PROCEDURE

1. **Where do you like to have breakfast? Sometimes it is nice to have breakfast in bed. Let's make breakfast in bed for some people in our families.** Invite students to choose one or more family members for whom to make breakfast in bed. Give two cups to each student. Each student uses a marker to write the name of a family member on the outside of one cup. Student adds decorations around name, cutting shapes from wrapping paper or party napkins and gluing shapes around name.

2. Student applies a thin line of clear glue around the rim of his or her decorated cup. Student places decorated cup inside second cup. Allow glue to dry. Students make one double-thick cup for each family member they chose.

3. Each student places 1/3 cup oatmeal, 1/3 cup powdered milk, 1 teaspoon sugar and 12 raisins in a resealable plastic bag, one bag for each family member they chose. On self-adhesive labels, students write "Add one cup hot water, stir and enjoy!" and then place labels on bags.

4. Students take cups and bags home and plan a time to serve breakfast in bed to family members, serving juice or milk in the cups students made and oatmeal mix in bowls. (Optional: Also provide fruit for students to take home and add to breakfasts they serve.)

OPTIONS FOR YOUNGER STUDENTS

1. Instead of cutting out shapes, students decorate cups with stickers. Assist students as needed with printing names of family members.

2. Print self-adhesive labels ahead of time.

OPTION FOR OLDER STUDENTS

Students write notes to family members, telling what they appreciate about each person or telling a favorite Bible verse.

Calendar Encouragement

MATERIALS

- ○ sheets of 8½x11-inch (21.5x27.5-cm) paper
- ○ markers
- ○ ruler
- ○ photocopier
- ○ staplers
- ○ several calendars for the current or coming year
- ○ glue
- ○ 12x18-inch (30x45-cm) sheets of construction paper

PREPARATION

Draw a blank calendar grid on a sheet of paper and photocopy 12 grids for each student.

PROCEDURE

1. **Encouraging family members is something we can do all year long. Let's make calendars and write encouraging messages for our families on each month.** Distribute 12 calendar grids to each student. Each student stacks pages together and staples along top edge of grids. Provide several calendars for the current or coming year. Student fills in month names and dates on his or her calendar and writes in special days such as birthdays, holidays and anniversaries. Student then writes encouraging messages for different members of his or her family in different calendar squares (at least one message for each month). Lead students in brainstorming encouraging messages as needed. ("Mom, thank you for helping me with my science project last year." "Bobby, you are a great soccer player." "Anna, my friends think you are cool." "Grandma, I like playing video games with you." "Dad, you are a great cook.")

2. Students glue finished calendars onto construction paper and then draw pictures of their homes or family members to decorate calendar backing (see sketch).

OPTIONS FOR YOUNGER STUDENTS

1. Students fill in only one month.
2. Help students write short messages on calendar pages as needed.

OPTION FOR OLDER STUDENTS

In various calendar squares, students write at least five things they appreciate about each member of their families. Students also write ways they can show love to family members (bring breakfast in bed, do extra chores, etc.). Students do these things on the days they chose.

Good-for-Something Coupon

MATERIALS

○ Coupon Patterns (p. 17)   ○ construction paper
○ photocopier   ○ scissors
○ paper   ○ markers
                         ○ glitter glue

PREPARATION

Photocopy one Coupon Patterns page for each student.

TO: Mom

FROM: Jill

GOOD FOR: one time of cleaning the table!

PROCEDURE

1. **Have you ever received coupons for (a local fast-food restaurant)? What were the coupons good for?** Volunteers respond. **A coupon is just a piece of paper, but you can exchange it for something else. What is a way you might help someone at home this week?** Ask questions to help students think of such things as putting away clothes, making beds, setting the table, stacking newspaper, playing other person's favorite board game for one hour, etc. After students tell answers, distribute pattern pages. Students choose one or more of the ways to help others at home, write the ways on the coupons and then cut out coupons and glue them to slightly larger squares of construction paper. Students decorate coupons with markers and glitter glue. **To whom will you give your coupon? What help does that person need? What can you do to help?**

2. After students complete coupons, invite volunteers to tell about their coupons. Close activity in prayer, leading students to ask for God's help in doing good things for their families.

TEACHING TIPS

1. In conversation during this activity, avoid making assumptions about a student's family life. For example, include natural references to students who live in blended families or foster families or who visit noncustodial parents, etc.

2. Talk with students about ways they can help a family member who doesn't live with them. Students might suggest writing letters, recording letters on audiocassettes or videotapes, praying for the person, etc.

3. Provide stickers or stamps and stamp pads for students to use in decorating coupons.

OPTION FOR YOUNGER STUDENTS

On a large sheet of paper, print ideas for what to write on coupons. Students choose what they want to write and then copy from paper.

OPTION FOR OLDER STUDENTS

Students make booklets of coupons—one coupon for each member of the family—or students may wish to make coupons for friends.

Coupon Patterns

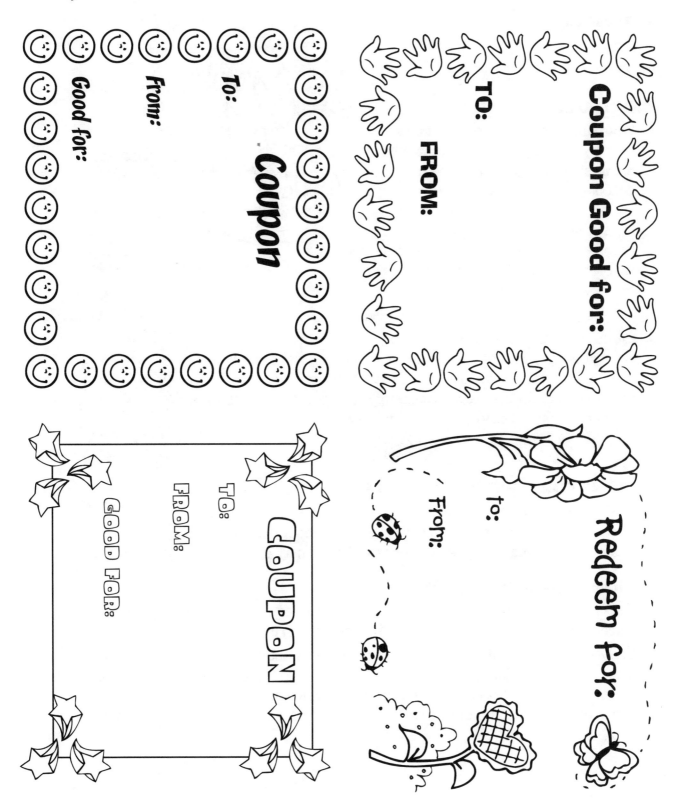

To:

From:

Good for:

Coupon

TO:

FROM:

Coupon Good for:

TO:

FROM:

GOOD FOR:

COUPON

to:

From:

Redeem for:

Secret Service

MATERIALS
- paper
- pencils
- postage stamps
- envelopes

PROCEDURE

1. **What are some ways you can serve God by showing love to your family members or neighbors?** (Send an encouraging card. Do your brother's chores. Make your parents' bed. Wash the car. Mow a neighbor's yard. Leave flowers for an elderly neighbor. Weed the garden.) Encourage students to think about ways to do these things secretly.

2. Each student chooses a secret service plan.

3. Group students in pairs or trios. Give paper and pencils to each group. Students describe their secret service plans to each other. Each student writes a reminder note to one other student in the pair or trio. Collect notes and mail them to students. Students perform their secret service acts during the week.

OPTIONS FOR YOUNGER STUDENTS

Invite volunteers to help you write a letter to be sent as a reminder of the secret service plan. Students decorate envelopes. Photocopy one letter for each student, place letters in decorated envelopes and mail letters to students during the week.

OPTIONS FOR OLDER STUDENTS

1. Students create secret codes in which to write reminder letters (A=C, B=D, etc.). Students write letters in their secret codes and include key for breaking the code.

2. Use yarn to divide a bulletin board into three sections. Label sections "Secret Mission," "In Progress," "Mission Completed." Students draw symbols or pictures on halves of index cards to represent their secret plans and place in the "Secret Mission" section. Each week, students move index cards to appropriate section until all cards are in the "Mission Completed" section.

Thank-You Cards

MATERIALS

○ 3x8½-inch (7.5x21.5-cm)
  strips of colored paper

○ scissors
○ markers

PROCEDURE

1. Ask each student to think of the people he or she lives with and one or two reasons he or she is thankful for each one. Invite volunteers to tell their responses.

2. Each student chooses a family member for whom to make a thank-you card. Give each student a strip of colored paper. Students cut and fold paper as shown (see sketch). Students write thank-you messages and decorate cards with markers.

3. **Write the person's name on the outside of the card and leave it for the person to find.** Encourage students to put cards in unusual places at home (on a pillow, in a favorite cup, on the bathroom mirror, on the TV, in a favorite book, etc.).

OPTION FOR YOUNGER STUDENTS

Cut and prefold cards.

OPTIONS FOR OLDER STUDENTS

1. Purchase origami paper (available at craft stores) to use in making colorful folding cards.

2. Provide a variety of materials to use for decorating (metallic markers and other unusual writing tools, stickers, paint, glitter, magazines from which to cut pictures and letters, etc.).

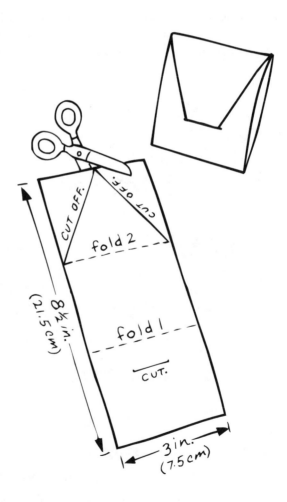

Welcome Box

MATERIALS

- ○ Phone List and Favorite Spots pages (pp. 21-22)
- ○ photocopier
- ○ paper
- ○ phone book
- ○ markers
- ○ large box
- ○ items for box (see first Teaching Tip)

PREPARATION

Find the name of a family who is new to your neighborhood and make arrangements to deliver box. Photocopy Phone List page. Photocopy at least one Favorite Spots page for each student.

PROCEDURE

1. **What do you think it is like to move to a new neighborhood?** Invite students who have recently moved to tell some of their experiences. **Today we are going to make a box filled with items to welcome a new family to our neighborhood.** Students use phone book to fill in the Phone List page with names and phone numbers. On Favorite Spots pages, students draw pictures or write about their favorite places to eat and favorite activities in the community and at your church. Students may also want to create and include in the box, maps of the inside of their school or a local mall or park.

2. Students use markers to decorate a large box and fill it with papers students prepared and items you provided.

TEACHING TIPS

1. Suggested items for Welcome Box: local street map, laundry soap, clothes hangers, breakfast bars or other packaged foods, paper towels, toilet paper, light bulbs, picture-hanging kits, batteries, stickers, coloring books, markers, etc.

2. After box is assembled, lead students in prayer for the people who will receive it.

3. If you have a large class, divide class into smaller groups and make several boxes.

OPTION FOR YOUNGER STUDENTS

Fill in the information on the Phone List ahead of time and photocopy list if you will be making more than one box.

OPTION FOR OLDER STUDENTS

Make an audiocassette or videotape with different students completing the following sentence starters: "My favorite place to eat is . . ."; "One fun place to go after school is . . ."; "On the weekends, my family likes to . . ."; "One thing I like to do at (church name) is . . ."; "I like to come to church because . . ."

Phone List

Welcome to the neighborhood! Here are some phone numbers that might be helpful.

UTILITIES

Phone: _____   Gas: _____

Electric: _____   Water/Sewer: _____

Trash: _____

SCHOOLS

Elementary schools: _____

Middle schools: _____

High schools: _____

EMERGENCY NUMBERS

Police: _____

Fire: _____

Hospital: _____

OTHER IMPORTANT NUMBERS

Library: _____

Recreation center: _____

Post office: _____

Church: _____

Favorite Spots

Absentee Cards

MATERIALS

- ⃝ blank postcards
- ⃝ markers
- ⃝ postage stamps

PROCEDURE

1. Distribute materials to students. Students draw pictures and write messages on blank postcards (see sketch) for students who have been absent. To help students think of what to draw or write ask, **What could you say to invite (Nathan and Diego) to come back to our class next week? What picture can you draw to show something you enjoy doing in our class?**

2. Students address and stamp completed postcards. During the week, mail postcards.

OPTIONS FOR YOUNGER STUDENTS

1. Students draw pictures or dictate messages for you to write.

2. Provide a variety of stickers for students to use to decorate cards.

OPTIONS FOR OLDER STUDENTS

1. Invite volunteers to suggest appropriate slogans for cards.

2. Instead of blank postcards, give students card stock and decorative-edged scissors. Students cut card stock into 3x5-inch (7.5x12.5-cm) rectangles to create cards to send to absentees. Students make as many cards as time permits.

3. Students make cards with "Sorry you missed the fun" on the front. On the back of cards, students copy jokes from joke books or write messages telling something fun that happened in class.

ENRICHMENT IDEA

Students tape-record or videotape messages telling what they enjoyed about their class. Students may also include some favorite music or Bible verses. Reproduce the tape and send copies to absentees.

New-Kid-at-Church Kit

MATERIALS

- ○ large sheet of paper
- ○ markers
- ○ shoe boxes (one for each group of three or four students)
- ○ paper
- ○ variety of items to place in each box (brochures describing children's activities at church, Bibles, maps of your church, candy bars, coupons for treats at local stores, audiocassette of music used in your class, etc.)

PROCEDURE

1. **When have you been to a new class or school? How do you think new kids or visitors feel when they come to our class?** Invite students to tell what they might need to know in order to feel welcome in a new class. (Names of the teachers and other students. Directions to the class. Directions to the closest bathroom and water fountain.) List students' ideas on a large sheet of paper.

2. Divide class into groups of three or four students. Students in each group work together to write welcome notes introducing themselves and telling helpful information. (Students refer to list on large sheet of paper as needed.)

3. Give each group a box and the items you collected to place in boxes. Students decorate boxes and place collected items and welcome notes inside.

TEACHING TIPS

1. After boxes are assembled, lead students in prayer for the people who will receive them.

2. Keep boxes in your classroom and give them to new students who come to your class throughout the year.

OPTION FOR YOUNGER STUDENTS

Invite volunteers to help you write a welcome letter for new students.

OPTION FOR OLDER STUDENTS

Students make audiocassettes telling about their class.

Postcard Pals

MATERIALS

○ Bibles
○ markers
○ blank adhesive address labels

○ scissors
○ paper bag
○ large sheet of paper
○ 4x7-inch (10x17.5-cm) card stock

○ a variety of decorating materials (ribbon, stickers, glitter, glue)
○ postage stamps

PREPARATION

Write each student's name and address on an address label. Cut labels apart and put them into the paper bag.

PROCEDURE

1. **What are some things you could say to encourage a kid your age in a difficult situation?** (God keeps His promises. God cares for you.) **What are some Bible verses that might be encouraging to know?** (Joshua 1:9. Psalm 139:14. John 3:16.) Print students' ideas on a large sheet of paper.

2. Give each student a blank postcard and decorating materials you have collected. Students write encouraging messages, referring to large sheet of paper for ideas. Then students decorate and stamp postcards.

3. Each student then secretly picks an address label from the paper bag and places it on postcard. During the week, mail postcards to the students.

TEACHING TIPS

1. To be sure every student in the group will receive a postcard, make up a message yourself. Then if a student does not complete his or her postcard, send yours instead. The students will enjoy having you participate in the activity.

2. Some students may make more than one encouraging message card. Send extras to students who may be absent.

OPTION FOR YOUNGER STUDENTS

Students draw pictures of Bible story events instead of writing messages to secret pals.

OPTION FOR OLDER STUDENTS

Students choose address labels before writing messages. Then as part of their messages, students tell several things that they like about their secret pals.

Church Family

Church Family

Things to Do on Your Own for Your Church Family

MATERIALS
- ⭕ Things You Can Do at Church page (p. 29)
- ⭕ photocopier
- ⭕ paper
- ⭕ index cards
- ⭕ scissors
- ⭕ markers
- ⭕ glue
- ⭕ hole punch
- ⭕ ribbon or yarn

PREPARATION
Photocopy Things You Can Do at Church page, one for each student.

PROCEDURE
1. Give each student eight index cards and a photocopied page. Students cut out ideas and glue each one onto a separate index card. Students use markers to decorate cards. Students punch two holes at the top of each index card and tie cards together with ribbon or yarn (see sketch).

2. Encourage each student to take his or her cards home and choose one or more ideas to do with his or her family.

OPTION FOR YOUNGER STUDENTS
Each student chooses one of the ideas from Things You Can Do at Church page to cut out, glue to index card and decorate. Encourage students to use the idea during the week.

OPTION FOR OLDER STUDENTS
Students suggest additional things they can do to help others in the church. Print students' ideas on a large sheet of paper. Each student chooses two or three additional ideas from large sheet of paper and writes ways on index cards.

ENRICHMENT IDEAS
1. Students keep a card file of ideas for serving others at church (p. 29), in the community (p. 65) and around the world (p. 107).

2. Students read idea cards at a family mealtime and challenge other family members to try one or more of the ideas on the cards. Families work together to see how many of their chosen ideas they can complete in one week.

Introduce yourself to new kids who come to your classroom.

Things You Can Do at Church

Try some of these ideas on your own!

Pick up papers left in the sanctuary after church services.	Introduce yourself to new kids who come to your classroom.
Ask your teacher if you can help clean up after class time.	**Help visitors find classrooms.**
Tell your pastor or music director what you like about church services.	Send thank-you notes to Sunday School teachers from previous years.
Pray for your pastor and Sunday School teachers.	**Put on a puppet show for a younger class.**

Garden Project

MATERIALS

○ materials and tools needed
   to complete project.

PREPARATION

Ask the person responsible for landscaping your church property to help you plan one or more gardening projects students can complete (plant annuals for a border, plant grass in an eroded area, rake up leaves or grass clippings, etc.). Notify students to wear clothing suitable for this project or provide old shirts to cover students' clothes.

PROCEDURE

Why do you think people plant trees and flowers? (They look nice. They help produce oxygen.) **Let's do a project to help care for (or plant) some plants around our church.** Briefly describe the gardening project you have planned. Give each student (or pair of students) a specific job to complete.

TEACHING TIPS

1. Take before-and-after pictures of the area in which students are working. You may also want to take pictures (photographs or videos) of children as they work on their service project. Display the photos or show the video in your classroom or a public area at your church.

2. If you have a large class or you teach alone, invite several parents to join your class for this activity.

OPTION FOR OLDER STUDENTS

Older students can participate in more challenging projects such as planting trees, shoveling snow, trimming shrubs or weeding.

Toy Shine!

MATERIALS

- ○ buckets of warm soapy water
- ○ sponges
- ○ paper towels
- ○ toys from church preschool rooms

PROCEDURE

Students wash and dry preschool toys. If some classrooms are not in use, students may also wash tables and chairs and larger toys such as plastic indoor slides, etc. **Your work will help young children stay healthy. Because young children put most things in their mouths, it is important to keep their toys as germ free as possible.**

TEACHING TIP

Take pictures of students as they clean. (If rooms are in poor condition, also take before and after pictures.) Display pictures outside of classroom.

OPTION FOR YOUNGER STUDENTS

Divide class into smaller groups, one group for each adult helper you have. Assign a different cleaning job to each group. Groups may wash toys, arrange books, sort crayons, wash tables and chairs, etc.

OPTION FOR OLDER STUDENTS

If needed, students can also vacuum the carpet, mop the floor and arrange blocks and other play areas in classrooms.

ENRICHMENT IDEA

If your church is planning to remodel nursery or preschool rooms, involve students and their families in the work. Students and parents can work together to paint, clean carpets, arrange furniture and decorate the walls.

Trash Collectors

MATERIALS
○ trash bags
○ heavy-duty gloves

PROCEDURE
Why do you think it is important to clean up trash? (Animals might get hurt. People might step on something sharp. Trash can smell bad.) **Let's look around our church to find trash that needs to be cleaned up.** Give trash bags to groups of two or three students. Students wear gloves as they collect trash from church parking lot or anywhere on the church grounds. Students wash hands at the end of the activity.

TEACHING TIP
Students work in groups of four to six. Assign one adult helper to each group to supervise the activity and make sure students pick up trash safely. If you do not have enough adult helpers, ask several parents to help with the activity.

OPTION FOR OLDER STUDENTS
Students collect trash in a nearby park or community area.

ENRICHMENT IDEA
Find out about recycling opportunities in your area (curbside recycling, aluminum-can redemption machines, glass recycling center, etc.). Students decorate and label a different bag or box for each item you want to recycle. Students sort trash they collect and place items in the appropriate bags or boxes.

Be-Wise Bookmarks

MATERIALS

○ Bibles   ○ scissors   ○ clear Con-Tact paper   ○ stickers
○ poster board   ○ ruler   ○ markers

PREPARATION

Cut poster board into 2½x8-inch (6.5x20.5-cm) strips—at least one for each student. Cut clear Con-Tact paper into 3x9-inch (7.5x23-cm) strips—two for each student. Arrange to give bookmarks to another class.

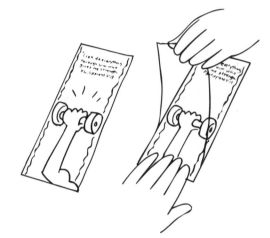

PROCEDURE

1. Explain to students that they will make bookmarks to give to another class as a way of helping the other students remember God's Word. Tell students about the class to whom they will be giving the bookmarks.

2. Students use Bibles to locate and read several Bible verses (see ideas in Teaching Tip below). Students tell the main ideas of the verses they read. Each student chooses a verse to write on a bookmark.

3. Distribute poster-board strips. Students write verses and decorate with markers and stickers to make bookmarks. Students cover both sides of strips with clear Con-Tact paper.

4. Lead students in prayer for the recipients of the bookmarks and then take students with you to deliver the bookmarks to the other class.

TEACHING TIP

Select Bible verses that go with the topic you are teaching or use some of the following verses: Psalms 1:1-3; 46:1-3; 86:5; 130:7; Proverbs 11:25,28; Isaiah 40:31; John 3:16; Romans 8:28,38,39; Galatians 5:22,23; Ephesians 2:8,9; Philippians 1:6; 4:13.

OPTION FOR YOUNGER STUDENTS

Photocopy the Bookmark Verses page (p. 34) for each student. Students choose verses they want to use. Students cut out bookmarks and then decorate them. Help students cover bookmarks with clear Con-Tact paper.

OPTION FOR OLDER STUDENTS

Cut blank overhead transparencies into 2x5-inch (5x12.5-cm) strips, at least one for each student. Students use permanent markers to write verses on strips. Each student then places his or her strip on top of one clear Con-Tact strip (sticky side up) and sprinkles glitter and/or confetti on the strip. Student then covers the layers with another strip of clear Con-Tact paper.

Bookmark Verses

"God is our refuge and strength, an ever-present help in trouble."

—Psalm 46:1

"For God so loved the world that he gave his one and only Son, that whoever believes in him shall not perish but have eternal life."

—John 3:16

"The fruit of the Spirit is love, joy, peace, patience, kindness, goodness, faithfulness, gentleness and self-control. Against such things there is no law."

—Galatians 5:22,23

"I can do everything through him who gives me strength."

—Philippians 4:13

College Student Care Package

MATERIALS

○ materials for the projects of your choice (see options below)

○ mailing materials (boxes, labels, postage, etc.)

PREPARATION

Talk with church leaders to find out about young adults who have gone away to college from your church.

PROCEDURE

1. **Many young adults go to other cities or states to go to college. Sometimes those college students feel lonely because they are away from home. Today we are going to make care packages for (name of college students).** Tell students about the college students you have chosen. Then lead students to complete the projects you chose.

2. Once projects are complete, students pack items in boxes and address mailing labels. Mail boxes during the week.

GORP

In paper bowls, students mix together any combination of dry cereal, pretzels, carob or chocolate chips and raisins. Students fill resealable plastic bags with mixture.

DECORATED SUGAR COOKIES

Provide plain sugar cookies, plastic knives, frosting and sugar sprinkles in different colors, and plastic wrap. Collect empty plastic squeeze containers such as ketchup or mustard bottles to make no-mess frosting dispensers. Students decorate cookies with frosting and sprinkles and then wrap cookies in plastic wrap.

COMIC-STRIP COLLECTIONS

Provide comic-strip pages from newspapers. Include as many colored pages as possible. Students cut out their favorite comic strips and glue them onto sheets of paper. Punch holes in left margin of each sheet and tie together with yarn to make a book.

OPTION FOR YOUNGER STUDENTS

Students draw pictures to send to college students.

OPTION FOR OLDER STUDENTS

Students write individual letters to college students asking about college life and describing things that have happened recently at church.

Doorknob Hangers

MATERIALS
- ⭘ Bibles
- ⭘ Doorknob Hanger Pattern (p. 37)
- ⭘ card stock
- ⭘ photo copier
- ⭘ larger sheet of paper
- ⭘ markers
- ⭘ scissors
- ⭘ glitter
- ⭘ glue
- ⭘ clear Con-Tact paper

PREPARATION
Photocopy Doorknob Hanger Pattern onto card stock—one for each student.

PROCEDURE
1. **What are some Bible verses, sentences or phrases that could help tell others about Jesus?** (John 3:16. Romans 6:23. "Jesus loves you." "Trust in God because He cares for you.") Write students' ideas on a large sheet of paper.
2. Give each student a Doorknob Hanger Pattern page. Students cut out doorknob hangers. On hangers, students print verses, sentences or phrases from large sheet of paper and decorate the hangers with markers, stickers and/or glitter. Cover doorknob hangers with clear Con-Tact paper.
3. Students hang doorknob hangers on doors of other classrooms around the church.

OPTION FOR YOUNGER STUDENTS
If needed, cut out doorknob hangers before class. Be available to help students cover hangers with clear Con-Tact paper.

OPTION FOR OLDER STUDENTS
Students cut out Doorknob Hanger Pattern and use as a pattern to cut out two hanger shapes from clear Con-Tact paper. Each student peels paper backing from one hanger shape and, from construction paper, cuts letters to make messages about Jesus. Student arranges letters, other shapes, glitter and confetti on hanger shape and then covers it with the other hanger shape to make a transparent doorknob hanger.

Doorknob Hanger Pattern

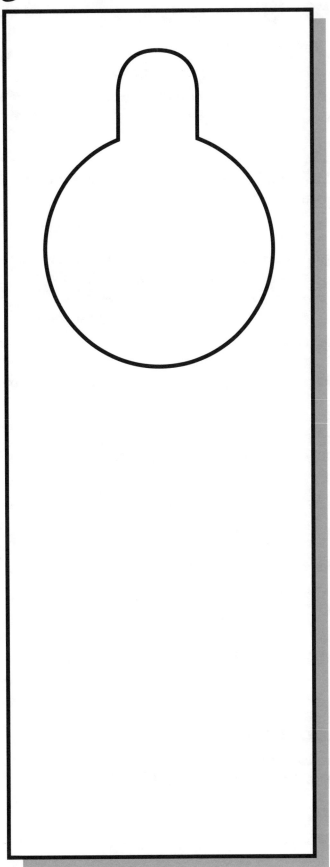

Encouraging Flyer

MATERIALS

○ Bibles
○ white paper
○ dark-colored markers or pens
○ colored paper
○ photocopier

PREPARATION

Get permission from your pastor or supervisor before placing flyers on cars or distributing them as people leave church.

PROCEDURE

1. Divide class into groups of two or three. Each group works together to think of a slogan that tells the main idea of Romans 8:35,37-39 ("Jesus is always near." "God's love is stronger than anything!" "God's love rules!") or John 3:16 ("God's love is for everyone!" "Believe in Jesus because He loves you!") or other Bible passage you are studying.

2. Distribute white paper and markers or pens. Students letter slogans on paper and illustrate the slogans to make flyers. Students include Bible references and name of class and church. Photocopy flyers on colorful paper and have students place them on cars in church parking lot or distribute as people leave church.

TEACHING TIPS

1. Putting into words what we believe usually helps us understand and internalize what it is that we truly believe.

2. Often students don't feel like significant members of God's family. By allowing them to share their faith and beliefs with others, you will be helping your students realize that they can contribute to the family of God.

3. When distributing flyers, make sure students are properly supervised. Make sure you have at least one teacher or adult helper for every eight students.

OPTION FOR YOUNGER STUDENTS

Print slogan suggestions for flyers on a large sheet of paper. Students copy onto their papers the slogans they want to use.

OPTION FOR OLDER STUDENTS

Students work together to make flyers that tell how to become a member of God's family (for ideas, refer to Evangelism Booklet on pp. 111-116).

ENRICHMENT IDEA

Students take flyers home and pass them out to friends in their neighborhoods.

Outside-In Party

MATERIALS

○ materials for the party ideas of your choice (see ideas below)

PREPARATION

Invite a younger class of students to a brief party hosted by your students at the end of the class time.

PROCEDURE

Students brainstorm party plans for a younger class and work together to prepare several party ideas (see ideas below or use ideas students think of). Lead students in praying for the younger class before the party. When younger class arrives, students work together to lead games, play music and/or serve food to the younger children.

Spoons

GAME

Students think of a game they enjoy playing (Duck, Duck, Goose; Steal the Bacon; Hot Potato; etc.) to teach to younger students, choosing who will give instructions and direct the game time. Students write directions on paper and rehearse how they will lead the game.

MUSIC

Students create simple musical instruments to give to younger students to use while listening to favorite praise or Scripture songs. During party, students demonstrate how to use instruments and allow younger students to use them.

Spoons: Tape together the handles of two metal spoons with spoons back-to-back. To play, hit spoons against palm of hand.

Shakers: Put uncooked beans, pasta, and/or small paper clips inside a sealable tube (empty tennis ball can or potato chip can). Cover end with lid. Tape lid shut. To play, shake or tilt tube back and forth.

FOOD

Students cut up a variety of fruits, spoon pieces into small paper cups and top with whipped cream or flavored yogurt. Provide plastic spoons and napkins for guests to use while eating snack. Also provide water or fruit juice to drink.

DECORATIONS

Students create a banner welcoming younger class to their party. Students also decorate room with balloons, streamers, etc. Students may use construction paper and markers to make welcome cards for students in younger class or make place mats on which to serve a snack.

OPTION FOR YOUNGER STUDENTS

Students only prepare food and decoration party ideas.

Play Dough Fun

MATERIALS

○ ingredients and utensils
  for the play dough recipe
  of your choice
  (see recipes below)

○ wax paper
○ airtight container

PREPARATION

Make arrangements to give play dough to a younger class.

PROCEDURE

Students wash hands before and after making play dough. Divide class into groups of no more than six. Students in each group work together to make play dough for a younger class (each recipe makes enough dough for six to eight students). Students measure ingredients and take turns mixing and kneading the dough. Add more water or flour as needed for desired consistency. As time permits, students play with the dough on wax paper and then place dough in an airtight container.

SALT-AND-FLOUR DOUGH

Students mix together 1½ cups flour, 1 cup cornstarch and 1 cup salt. Add 1 cup warm water and several drops of food coloring. Students take turns kneading the dough until soft and pliable.

KOOL-AID DOUGH

In a large bowl, students mix together 2½ cups flour, ½ cup salt and 2 packages dry unsweetened Kool-Aid. In a small bowl, students mix 2 cups boiling water with 3 tablespoons cooking oil. Students pour liquid mixture into dry ingredients and stir until mixture forms a ball. As mixture cools, students take it out of the bowl and knead it until soft and pliable.

CORNMEAL DOUGH

In a large bowl, students mix together 1 cup water, 1 cup salt, 1½ cups flour, 1½ cups cornmeal. Students take turns kneading the dough until soft and pliable.

TEACHING TIP

Make one batch of dough for each group of no more than six students. Vary different batches of play dough using some of the following ideas:

• Add several drops of food coloring to make each batch a different color.

• Add ¼ cup instant coffee to vary the texture of the dough.

• Add cinnamon or a drop of perfume or flavoring extract to play dough before kneading.

Record a Story

MATERIALS

○ one or more Bible storybooks
○ audiocassette recorder
○ blank audiocassette
○ bell
○ one or more resealable plastic bags (large enough for a storybook and cassette)
○ permanent marker

PREPARATION

Arrange to borrow one or more Bible storybooks from the teacher of a class of three-, four- or five-year-olds. Arrange for a time when your students may deliver storybook recordings to the younger class.

PROCEDURE

1. Students choose a Bible story to record. Students practice reading the story. **What might a child learn from this story?** Assign each student a page or two of the story to read, ringing the bell when it is time to turn the page. Encourage students to read with expression in their voices to make the story interesting and lively.

2. Record story, beginning with the title and saying, "Turn the page when you hear the bell." Students place cassette and book in a resealable plastic bag, label the bag with the book name and give the bag to a class of younger children.

TEACHING TIPS

1. Instead of a bell, another rhythm instrument such as a shaker or triangle or tambourine can be used.

2. If you have a large group, divide class into several groups. Each group makes a separate Bible story tape. Provide several audiocassette recorders, blank audiocassettes and Bible storybooks.

OPTION FOR YOUNGER STUDENTS

Read the story aloud to students. Students plan sound effects to make during the story. Practice reading the story with students' sound effects several times. Then record story and sound effects.

OPTION FOR OLDER STUDENTS

Students add appropriate sound effects to the story, and different students read each character's dialogue, reading the story like a play.

ENRICHMENT IDEA

Instead of making an audiocassette, bring a video camera and videotape students reading the story. Focus the camera on the pictures as students read.

Reminder Bands

MATERIALS

- ○ fine-tip markers
- ○ letter-size paper in a variety of bright colors
- ○ rulers
- ○ scissors
- ○ pencils
- ○ glue
- ○ a 12-inch (30-cm) length of leather lacing or fishing line for each student
- ○ optional—assorted plastic beads

PREPARATION

Arrange to give bands to a group of younger students.

PROCEDURE

1. Explain that students will be making bands for younger children to wear as reminders of ways to obey God's Word. Bands may be worn around ankles or wrists, or children may hang them in their rooms.

2. Distribute materials to students. Students measure and cut colored paper rectangles approximately 4x¾ inches (10x1.9 cm). Each student should make four to six rectangles.

3. At one end of each rectangle, students use markers to write words on the rectangles reminding them of ways to obey God's Word, one word on each rectangle (see sketch).

4. Have students make paper beads by doing the following: Roll each paper rectangle around a pencil (see sketch) so that the word remains readable. Place a small amount of glue under the end and roll tightly. Hold the rectangle in place around the pencil for a few seconds. Then slide the bead off the pencil. Set aside to dry.

5. After making paper beads, students thread them onto the leather lacing or fishing line and tie and trim the ends. (Optional: Students also thread assorted plastic beads onto their bands.)

6. Students deliver bands to a group of younger students.

TEACHING TIPS

1. Make a sample band before class. Wear the band around your wrist during class.
2. For fast drying, use glue sticks.
3. String, raffia, narrow ribbon or twine can also be used to make the bands.

OPTION FOR YOUNGER STUDENTS

Measure and cut paper for students before class. Students each make only one paper bead.

OPTION FOR OLDER STUDENTS

Students make bands with beads that create a sentence: "Jesus loves you!" "God cares for you." "Be a part of God's family."

Snack Share

MATERIALS

○ ingredients and utensils for the recipe of your choice (see recipe ideas on pp. 44-45)

PREPARATION

Contact another class and arrange to bring a snack to share near the end of class time.

PROCEDURE

1. Students wash hands. Provide ingredients for students to make a snack to share with another class. Give each student or group of students a job to do to help prepare the snack (wash table, mix ingredients, count out napkins, carry snack to other class, etc.).

2. As students work, tell them about the class to whom they will be taking the snack. **What are some things we can do or say to encourage the students in this class?** (Serve the other class before serving own class. Smile and introduce selves to people in other class. Sit with people you haven't met before and talk with them.) Students deliver snack and eat snack with that class.

TEACHING TIPS

1. Students may use paper plates as trays to carry the snack to the other class.

2. Giving each student a "place mat" of wax paper will make cleanup easier.

3. Check to make sure that children eating the snack have no food allergies or restrictions.

ENRICHMENT IDEA

Students make a large amount of Gorp or Rice Cake Treats and store snacks in resealable plastic bags. Take snacks to a shelter or tutoring center.

Recipes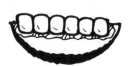

APPLE SMILES

Cut apples into lengthwise slices. For each snack, student spreads peanut butter on an apple slice and then sticks miniature marsh-mallows to the peanut butter to make toothy smiles (see sketch).

BANANA SANDWICHES

Using plastic knives, students cut peeled bananas into thin slices. Students put each slice of banana between two vanilla wafers.

EDIBLE ANIMALS

Provide dried fruit, miniature marshmallows and toothpicks. Each student makes two or more animals from these items.

BRAN BALLS

In a large mixing bowl, students combine ½ cup peanut butter and ¼ cup honey. Students take turns to stir in ½ cup apple juice and 3 cups raisin bran cereal. Students shape one tablespoon of mixture at a time into a ball and roll ball in chopped nuts. Recipe serves 12 to 14 people.

FRUIT SNACK

Provide a variety of fresh fruit, several knives and cutting boards. Students wash and cut up fruit to make a fruit salad. Students spoon fruit salad into paper cups. Top with flavored yogurt if desired.

Recipes

RICE CAKE TREATS

Students spread softened cream cheese or peanut butter on rice cakes and then use raisins to make happy faces on the rice cakes.

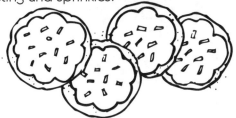

DECORATED SUGAR COOKIES

Bring plain sugar cookies, plastic knives, different colors of frosting and sugar sprinkles. Collect empty plastic squeeze containers such as ketchup or mustard bottles to make no-mess frosting dispensers. Students decorate cookies with frosting and sprinkles.

INDOOR S'MORES

Students spread marshmallow frosting on graham crackers, place sections of chocolate candy bar on the frosting and top with additional graham crackers.

BANANA PUDDING

Students put granola mix in bottom of small paper cups. Students slice bananas with a plastic knife and put a few slices in each cup. Students make instant pudding and then add pudding to cups.

BANANA BUGS

Students poke pretzel sticks into peeled whole bananas to make legs and antennae. To make spines and eyes, students use peanut butter to attach chocolate chips.

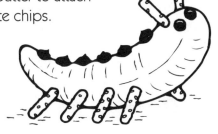

GORP

In paper bowls, students mix together any combination of dry cereal, pretzels, carob or chocolate chips and raisins. Students fill plastic sandwich bags with mixture.

Story of Thanks

MATERIALS

○ Bibles
○ construction paper
○ scissors
○ glue
○ fine-tip markers
○ good-quality paper towels
○ flannel board
○ optional—fabric scraps, fabric trim

PREPARATION

Arrange for your class to present a brief Bible story to a class of preschool children. Choose one of the Bible stories listed in Teaching Tips or another short and simple Bible story.

PROCEDURE

1. Students read aloud Bible story you chose. Lead students to review and discuss the story they read. **Who are the main characters in the story? What did these people do? What did they learn? What can we learn about God and how He wants us to live from this story?**

2. Students make flannel figures for the Bible story. To make figures, have students do the follow-  ing: Cut triangles of any color construction paper for bodies. Cut circles for faces. Glue the circles to the top of the triangles and draw faces, hair and clothing (see sketch). (Optional: Glue fabric scraps or fabric trim to triangle for clothing.) Cut paper towels to fit backs of figures. Glue paper-towel pieces to backs of construction-paper figures to make figures stick to flannel board.

3. While one student reads Bible story aloud, volunteers practice moving figures as the story action indicates. Students present story to a preschool class.

TEACHING TIPS

1. Use one of the following Bible stories: Mark 4:35-40; 12:41-44; Luke 7:11-17; 10:30-37; 10:38-42; 17:11-19; 18:35-43; 19:1-9.

2. Instead of paper towels, glue strips of sandpaper to backs of figures. Sandpaper will adhere to flannel boards more securely.

3. Students make flannel boards by gluing pieces of felt or flannel to the insides of box lids.

OPTIONS FOR OLDER STUDENTS

1. Invite several students to write a script for the story. Other students make flannel figures or pre-pare popcorn and juice to serve to the preschoolers.

2. Instead of flannel figures, students make puppets following directions and patterns on pages 101-102 or 121-122.

Trustworthy Posters

MATERIALS

- ◯ Bibles
- ◯ paper
- ◯ pencils
- ◯ poster board
- ◯ tape
- ◯ a variety of decorating materials (markers, metallic pens, poster paints, brushes, fabric scraps, glue, construction paper scraps, glitter, etc.)

PROCEDURE

1. Divide class into groups of two or three and give each group paper and a pencil. Assign each group one of the following Bible verses: Psalm 136:1; 145:18; Isaiah 40:31; Romans 8:38,39; Philippians 4:13. More than one group may have the same verse. **According to these verses, what reasons do we have to trust God?** Allow groups time to read Bible verses and write down reasons to trust God.

2. Students use poster board to make posters that illustrate their assigned verses. Students write verse (or key words or phrases from the verse) and use materials you provide to decorate their posters. Display completed posters on walls of church facility, or display posters together on a large bulletin board. Title the bulletin-board display "Trust God Because …"

TEACHING TIPS

1. Provide scratch paper on which students sketch their poster ideas.

2. If students are having difficulty thinking of poster ideas ask, **How would you say the words of the verse you read in your own words? What's the most important idea this verse talks about?**

OPTION FOR YOUNGER STUDENTS

Discuss reasons to trust God. On a large sheet of paper, list reasons that students suggest. Students choose words or phrases from the list and copy them on poster board and then decorate the posters.

OPTION FOR OLDER STUDENTS

Divide class into groups of no more than six. Assign each group an area in your church in which to display their posters.

Verse Commercials

MATERIALS

○ Bibles   ○ paper

○ video camera   ○ markers

○ blank videotape

PREPARATION

Make arrangements to show commercials to another class of students, to students who were absent the day of the taping or in a public area at your church.

PROCEDURE

1. Divide class into groups of no more than six. Assign each group a Bible verse that tells about God's love and salvation (John 3:16; Romans 5:8; Ephesians 2:8,9; Titus 3:4,5), repeating references as needed. Groups read assigned verses and create a commercial to tell others about the verse. Students may read verse and show pictures that illustrate words of the verse, act out ways people respond when they believe the verse, sing the words of the verse to a familiar tune or make up motions for some of the words of the verse.

2. Groups practice their commercials several times. Groups take turns videotaping their commercials.

TEACHING TIPS

1. Make copies of the video for students to show to their families and friends.

2. Invite students who are reluctant to be in a commercial to run the camera or do special effects such as lighting or sound.

OPTION FOR YOUNGER STUDENTS

Instead of dividing class into groups, lead students to work together on a commercial that tells about John 3:16. Students can make up motions, make and show pictures, etc.

OPTION FOR OLDER STUDENTS

Provide large sheets of butcher paper, paint and brushes. Students choose background settings (park, classroom, street, etc.) and paint backdrops for their commercials.

ENRICHMENT IDEA

Show portions of the video during worship services or at a church function.

We've Got Rhythm

MATERIALS

○ materials for the instruments of your choice (see descriptions below)

PREPARATION

Make arrangements to visit a younger group at the end of a class time.

PROCEDURE

1. Students make one or more of the rhythm instruments. After instruments are made, practice singing a simple song to sing with children in a younger class ("Jesus Loves Me," "Jesus Loves the Little Children," etc.).

2. Talk with students about the class you will visit and how to interact with the younger children. Students bring instruments to younger class, give instruments to children and sing a song with them. (Note: If your class cannot visit a younger class, arrange to give instruments to the teacher for use in singing songs with the class.)

SHOEBOX GUITAR

Cut a 3-inch (7.5-cm) diameter hole in the center of a shoe-box lid. Put lid on box and stretch three large rubber bands around box lengthwise (see sketch). Cut plastic straws to 4-inch (10-cm) lengths. On each side of hole, 2 inches (5 cm) away, insert a straw under the rubber bands. Play by plucking strings.

RHYTHM TUBES

Cover a paper towel tube with colorful adhesive-backed paper or construction paper or decorate tube with stickers or markers. Play by tapping tubes together.

JINGLING BRACELETS

Thread four or five large jingle bells onto a length of chenille wire and twist wire to hold bells in place. Twist ends of wire together firmly and cover with a small piece of electrical tape. Children slip bell bracelets onto their arms and play by moving their arms.

OPTION FOR OLDER STUDENTS

Students make an audio or video recording of themselves singing several early childhood songs with which younger children may sing along as they use their musical instruments.

Bearing Fruit

MATERIALS
- Bibles
- index cards
- markers
- tissue paper
- baskets or sturdy gift bags with handles
- a variety of fruit
- glue
- a variety of decorating materials (ribbons, dried flowers, etc.)

PREPARATION
Make arrangements to deliver projects to shut-ins or elderly people in your church. Contact your pastor or other church leader for suggestions of people.

PROCEDURE
1. Read aloud Romans 8:35,37 or other verses about God's love. **What do these verses tell us about God's love? How do you think these verses might encourage some of the older people in our church?** Students tell ideas.

2. Divide class into groups of two or three. Give index cards and markers to each group. Guide groups to print Romans 8:35,37 or other verses about God's love on index cards. Students decorate cards with markers.

3. Each group puts several sheets of colorful tissue paper into a basket or bag and fills it with various fruits. Students decorate baskets or bags with various materials and insert cards they made.

TEACHING TIPS
1. Include plastic eggs filled with soft candy or nuts.
2. Use an instant camera to take pictures of students to include with the fruit. Notify parents ahead of time in order to obtain any permission needed for photos.

OPTION FOR YOUNGER STUDENTS
Print Bible verse on index cards before class. In class, students decorate cards and sign their names.

OPTION FOR OLDER STUDENTS
Students work together to write letters to basket recipients, telling recipients what they have been learning in class. Photocopy letters and include letters with each basket.

Bible Balloons

MATERIALS

○ Bibles
○ index cards
○ markers

○ hole punch
○ inflated balloons with thin
   ribbon streamers

○ optional—glitter, glue

PREPARATION

Arrange to deliver greeting cards to shut-ins, elderly people or others in your church who may be sick or lonely. Contact your pastor or other church leader for suggestions of people.

PROCEDURE

1. **What are some ways we can encourage others?** (Talk to them. Listen to them. Tell them about God's love. Give them something fun. Visit them.) **Let's make something to encourage some people from our church.** Give each student an index card. Student writes his or her name on one side of the card and copies Psalms 46:1, 52:8b or 118:6a onto the other side. Students draw colorful borders on cards (see sketch). (Optional: Students use glitter and glue to create sparkling borders.)

2. Each student punches a hole in a corner of his or her completed card. Student then threads ribbon through hole in the card and ties the card near the neck of the balloon.

OPTION FOR YOUNGER STUDENTS

Photocopy one Bible Verse Cards page (p. 54) for each student. Students cut out verses they want to use and glue verses to construction paper squares before attaching to balloons.

OPTION FOR OLDER STUDENTS

Use helium-filled balloons. Students create balloon bouquets, arranging several balloons with verse cards. Students tie ends of strings around small stuffed animal or candy container.

ENRICHMENT IDEA

Contact a local nursing home and ask if any residents will be celebrating birthdays in the coming month. Arrange to have students deliver balloon(s) to each person celebrating a birthday that month.

Birthday Box

MATERIALS

- ○ Bibles
- ○ shoe boxes
- ○ birthday wrapping paper
- ○ tape

- ○ butcher paper
- ○ markers
- ○ paper
- ○ cassette recorder

- ○ blank audiocassettes
- ○ balloons
- ○ streamers
- ○ ribbon

PREPARATION

Make arrangements to give birthday boxes to senior adults in your church family. Contact your pastor or other church leader for suggestions of people.

PROCEDURE

1. **Birthday parties are fun! Let's make some Birthday Boxes for some people in our church who might not have parties to celebrate their birthdays.** Divide class into groups of three or four. Students in each group work together to complete these tasks: Wrap a shoe box in birthday wrapping paper, wrapping the lid separately from the bottom. Make a banner with happy birthday wishes. Make and sign a birthday card.

2. Students in each group practice reading some favorite Bible verses (Psalms 91:1,2; 139:1-3; 146:7b-10; Romans 5:1; etc.). Tape-record students reading verses and singing "Happy Birthday to You." Each group makes one cassette.

3. Students pack boxes with balloons, streamers, cassettes and banners. Students tie the boxes closed with a bright ribbon and attach the cards.

OPTION FOR YOUNGER STUDENTS

Wrap shoe boxes before class and help students memorize one or two Bible verses to record.

OPTION FOR OLDER STUDENTS

Invite students to go with you to deliver each box and celebrate the senior's birthday.

ENRICHMENT IDEAS

1. Bring an instant camera and take pictures of students to include in boxes. Notify parents ahead of time in order to obtain any permission needed for photos.

2. Include a small wrapped present in each birthday box.

Greeting Cards

MATERIALS
- ○ Bible Verse Cards page (p. 54)
- ○ photocopier
- ○ paper
- ○ construction paper
- ○ markers
- ○ scissors
- ○ glue

PREPARATION
Arrange to deliver greeting cards to elderly shut-ins or others who may have to stay at home. Contact your pastor or other church leader for suggestions of people. Photocopy one Bible Verse Cards page for each student.

PROCEDURE

1. **Getting mail is always fun—especially if you're too sick to go out. Let's make greeting cards for some people from our church who have to stay at home.**

2. Distribute construction paper, Bible Verse Cards pages, markers, scissors and glue. Students fold construction paper in half and in half again to make cards (see sketches). Students choose Bible verses to cut out, color and glue inside greeting cards. Students then decorate fronts of cards and write personal messages.

OPTION FOR YOUNGER STUDENTS
Before class, on a large sheet of paper print several messages students could use on their cards. Students copy messages they want to use.

OPTION FOR OLDER STUDENTS
Provide card stock and decorative-edged scissors. Students create cards in a variety of shapes and sizes.

ENRICHMENT IDEA
Students choose one or more seniors in your church to adopt as grandparents. Invite the adopted grandparents to visit the class to tell stories. Give gifts class makes to the adopted grandparents and serve juice and cookies.

Bible Verse Cards

"Those who hope in the Lord will renew their strength. They will soar on wings like eagles; they will run and not grow weary, they will walk and not be faint."

Isaiah 40:31

"I am convinced that neither death nor life, neither angels nor demons, neither the present nor the future, nor any powers, neither height nor depth, nor anything else in all creation, will be able to separate us from the love of God that is in Christ Jesus our Lord."

Romans 8:38,39

"For as high as the heavens are above the earth, so great is his love for those who fear him."

Psalm 103:11

"You are forgiving and good, O Lord, abounding in love to all who call to you."

Psalm 86:5

Growing Gifts

MATERIALS

- Bible Verse Cards page (p. 54)
- photocopier
- paper
- newspaper
- markers

- scissors
- flowering plants
- potting soil
- pots

- trowels or large spoons
- materials to decorate pots (stickers, ribbons and glitter)
- glue
- craft sticks

PREPARATION

Arrange to deliver plants to elderly shut-ins or others who may be sick or lonely. Contact your pastor or other church leader for suggestions of people. Photocopy one Bible Verse Cards page for each student. Use newspaper to cover area where students will work.

PROCEDURE

1. **What would you need if you had to stay home all the time and could not go anywhere?** Students tell ideas. **Today we are going to make a gift for people who have to stay home a lot because of illness, lack of transportation or other reasons.**

2. Distribute materials. Each student chooses one or more of the verse cards. Students cut out cards and use markers to decorate them.

3. Provide flowering plants, potting soil, pots and trowels or large spoons. Students decorate pots using stickers, ribbons or glitter and then plant flowering plants in the decorated pots. Each student glues one of the verse cards to one end of a craft stick. Students put card sticks in soil near plant.

OPTION FOR YOUNGER STUDENTS

Purchase already potted small flowering plants. Each student places a potted plant on a square of colorful tissue paper and gathers paper up around edge of pot. Students tie tissue paper in place with ribbon. Students prepare cards as above.

OPTION FOR OLDER STUDENTS

Students write short letters to send with the plants, telling why they chose the verses they did. ("I wanted to give you Psalm 103:11 because it reminds me that God loves me, and I hope it reminds you of His love, too.")

ENRICHMENT IDEA

Invite students to go with you to deliver plants. Students practice one or more songs to sing when they give plants.

Refrigerator Magnets

MATERIALS
- ○ large sheet of paper
- ○ marker
- ○ 3-inch (7.5-cm) poster-board squares
- ○ fine-tip markers
- ○ 1-inch (2.5-cm) adhesive magnetic strips (available at craft stores)

PREPARATION
Arrange for magnets to be distributed to senior adults in your church.

3 in. (7.5 cm)

3 in. (7.5 cm)

PROCEDURE
1. Invite volunteers to tell ideas for pictures they could draw to cheer up others (sun, happy face, flowers, hearts). List students' ideas on a large sheet of paper. Students then suggest messages that are encouraging ("God loves you and always keeps His promises!" "God says that He will never leave you." "We care about you."). List these ideas on large sheet of paper along with picture ideas.

2. Explain that students will make encouraging magnets to give to senior adults in your church. Distribute poster-board squares and markers. Students draw pictures and write brief messages on the poster-board squares (see sketch).

3. Students attach magnetic strips to the backs of poster-board squares.

TEACHING TIP
If your church has a membership directory with photos, show pictures of the people who will receive the magnets.

OPTION FOR YOUNGER STUDENTS
Instead of writing messages, students cut out verses from Bible Verse Cards page (p. 54) and glue verses to poster board. Students trim poster board to the size of verse cards and color them.

OPTION FOR OLDER STUDENTS
Students use decorative-edged scissors to cut poster board into a variety of shapes. If possible, provide bright- or neon-colored poster board or other heavy paper for students to use.

ENRICHMENT IDEA
Take pictures (photographs or videos) of students as they work on their service project. Display the photos or show the video in your classroom or in a public area at your church.

Vine Designs

MATERIALS

- ○ newspaper
- ○ pliers
- ○ wire cutters
- ○ gravel
- ○ potting soil
- ○ large spoons
- ○ construction paper
- ○ markers
- ○ for each pair of students, bring one 4-inch (10-cm) flowerpot, a 30-inch (75-cm) long piece of 20-gauge wire, and one small ivy plant.

PREPARATION

Arrange to deliver plants to shut-ins or elderly people in your church. Contact your pastor or other church leader for suggestions of people. Cover work area with newspaper.

PROCEDURE

1. Divide class into pairs. Give each pair materials for making one potted plant. Pairs bend one end of the wire into a circle smaller than the bottom of the flowerpot (see sketch). Then pairs bend opposite end of wire into a simple shape such as a heart, bird or star. Students use wire cutters to trim ends as needed. Placing the circle end of the wire into the bottom of the pot, students cover it with gravel and then use large spoons to fill pot with soil. Students place ivy plant in pot near the wire and twist ivy around the wire.

2. Students make construction paper greeting cards to send with the ivy topiaries.

TEACHING TIPS

If you do not have ivy long enough to complete topiaries, students prepare wire and plant small ivy plants and take care of plants for several weeks, guiding plants to grow around wires. Deliver plants when they have grown enough to cover wires.

OPTION FOR YOUNGER STUDENTS

Prepare wire shapes before class.

Appreciation Party

MATERIALS

- ○ disposable wipes
- ○ plain sugar cookies
- ○ frosting
- ○ plastic knives
- ○ small candies
- ○ plates
- ○ napkins
- ○ balloons
- ○ streamers
- ○ butcher paper
- ○ markers
- ○ punch
- ○ cups
- ○ tape

PREPARATION

Before class, invite people who help in your church (pastors, music directors, volunteers for service groups, secretaries, etc.) to a party. Ask guests to arrive 10 to 15 minutes before the end of class time.

PROCEDURE

1. **Many people work to help care for the people in our church. Let's have a party to thank these people.** Divide class into three groups. Students in first group wash hands with disposable wipes and then frost cookies and decorate them with small candies. (Be sure to have enough cookies for guests and students as well.) Students place cookies on plates and arrange on table with napkins.

2. Second group of students decorates the classroom with balloons and streamers. Third group prints "Thank You" in large letters in the center of a long piece of butcher paper and decorates it to make a banner. All students write their names and thank-you messages around edges. Display banner in classroom.

3. When guests arrive, students greet them and serve cookies and punch.

TEACHING TIPS

1. If guests are not available during class time, send letters to parents ahead of time, asking them to allow students to stay 10 to 15 minutes after class. Ask guests to arrive as soon as class time is over.

2. Carefully supervise the students frosting cookies to be sure they do not lick fingers or knives.

OPTION FOR YOUNGER STUDENTS

Instead of writing messages on the butcher paper, students draw pictures of ways the invited guests help others. Students present pictures to guests during the party.

OPTION FOR OLDER STUDENTS

Students make individual thank-you cards for people who come to the party. In cards, students tell why they are glad guests help in the church.

Scent-sational Thanks

MATERIALS

- ○ loose-weave fabric (netting, tulle, muslin)
- ○ scissors
- ○ ruler
- ○ cut flowers (including roses and lavender)
- ○ small paper bags
- ○ powdered arrowroot (acts as a preservative)
- ○ potpourri oil (available at craft stores)
- ○ ribbon
- ○ construction paper
- ○ markers

PREPARATION

Cut fabric into 6-inch (15-cm) squares, one for each pair of students. Obtain a list of names of church staff or volunteers.

PROCEDURE

1. Divide class into pairs and distribute materials. Assign each pair of students the name of a staff member or volunteer. Invite students to tell reasons they are thankful for their assigned people.

2. Students pull the petals off the flowers and put them into their paper bags. Students sprinkle a little arrowroot into the bags. Then they close the bags and shake them for a while, dusting the petals with arrowroot. Students then put a drop of potpourri oil into each bag. Students shake bags again. Students pour their potpourri from the paper bags onto squares of fabric. Students gather fabric around potpourri and tie closed with a ribbon.

3. Students use construction paper and markers to make cards and write messages of thanks. Then students put the potpourri bags and cards in a place where staff members or volunteers will easily find them.

OPTION FOR YOUNGER STUDENTS

Before class, print "Thank you!" on slips of paper for each pair of students. Students color and decorate slips of paper instead of making cards.

OPTION FOR OLDER STUDENTS

Arrange with your pastor to allow older students to thank the staff member(s) or volunteers and present gift(s) in front of the congregation during a church service.

ENRICHMENT IDEA

Students make extra potpourri bags to take home and give as gifts to people they want to thank or to people they love.

Thank-You Nameplates

MATERIALS

- ○ construction paper
- ○ scissors
- ○ ruler
- ○ 8½x11 (21.5x27.5-cm) card stock
- ○ markers
- ○ stickers
- ○ glitter crayons

PREPARATION

Cut 3x5-inch (7.5x12.5-cm) slips of construction paper, one for each pair of students. Make a sample nameplate. Divide class into pairs and distribute materials. Assign each pair of students the name of a staff member.

PROCEDURE

1. Invite volunteers to tell reasons they are thankful for different people on the church staff. Show sample nameplate and tell students that they will be making nameplates to thank church staff for the help they give to people in the church. Distribute materials. Students work in pairs to make nameplates for church staff.

2. Students fold sheets of card stock in half lengthwise to make nameplates, one for each person on the church staff. Each pair carefully prints their assigned name onto both sides of the card. Students decorate nameplates with stickers, markers, and glitter crayons.

3. Each pair then writes a message of thanks on slips of paper and signs their names. Place the nameplates with slips of paper on the desks of the church staff or in a place were staff will easily find them.

TEACHING TIPS

1. If you have a small church staff, you may also wish to prepare thank-you gifts for volunteer leaders at your church.

2. For durability, cover construction paper nameplates with clear Con-Tact paper.

OPTION FOR YOUNGER STUDENTS

Before class, print church staff names and "Thank you!" on sheet of paper and photocopy for each pair of students. Students cut out message and their assigned name, glue to folded card stock and sign their names.

Wings of Thanks

MATERIALS

- ○ construction paper
- ○ scissors
- ○ ruler
- ○ Butterfly Pattern (p. 62)
- ○ photocopier
- ○ card stock
- ○ markers
- ○ craft sticks
- ○ glue
- ○ hole punch
- ○ ribbon or yarn

PREPARATION

Cut 3x5-inch (7.5x12.5-cm) slips of construction paper, one for each pair of students. Photocopy the Butterfly Pattern onto card stock. Make one pattern for each pair of students.

PROCEDURE

1. Divide class into pairs and distribute materials. Assign each pair of students the name of a staff member. Invite volunteers to tell reasons they are thankful for different people on the church staff.

2. Students cut out butterflies and color them with markers. Then students glue each butterfly to a craft stick (see sketch).

3. Each pair then writes "Thank you!" on slips of paper and signs their names. Pairs punch holes in slips of paper and butterflies and use ribbon or yarn to tie slips of paper to butterflies. Then deliver the butterflies to the church staff.

TEACHING TIP

If you have a small church staff, you may also wish to prepare thank-you gifts for volunteer leaders at your church.

OPTION FOR YOUNGER STUDENTS

Before class, print "Thank you!" on slips of paper for each pair of students. Students color and decorate slips of paper.

OPTION FOR OLDER STUDENTS

Arrange with your pastor to allow older students to thank the staff member(s) and present gift(s) in front of the congregation during a Sunday service.

Butterfly Pattern

Community

Community

Things to Do on Your Own for Your Community

MATERIALS

- Things You Can Do in Your Community page (p. 65)
- photocopier
- paper
- scissors
- index cards
- glue
- markers
- hole punch
- ribbon or yarn

PREPARATION

Photocopy Things You Can Do in Your Community page—one for each student.

PROCEDURE

1. Give each student seven index cards and a copy of the Things You Can Do in Your Community page. Students cut out ideas and glue each one onto a separate index card. Students use markers to decorate cards. Students punch two holes at the top of each index card and tie cards together with ribbon or yarn (see sketch).

2. Encourage each student to take his or her cards home and choose one idea to do with his or her family.

Clean up trash on sidewalks.

OPTION FOR YOUNGER STUDENTS

Each student chooses one of the ideas from Things You Can Do in Your Community page to cut out, glue to index card and decorate. Encourage students to use the idea during the week.

OPTION FOR OLDER STUDENTS

Students suggest additional things they can do to help others in the community. Print students' ideas on a large sheet of paper. Each student chooses two or three additional ideas from large sheet of paper and writes ways on index cards.

ENRICHMENT IDEAS

1. Students keep a card file of ideas for serving others in the community (p. 65), at church (p. 29) and around the world (p. 107).

2. Students read idea cards at a family mealtime and challenge other family members to try one or more of the ideas on the cards. Families work together to see how many of their chosen ideas they can complete in one week.

Things You Can Do in Your Community

Try some of these ideas on your own!

Pray for the leaders in your community.

Clean up trash on sidewalks.

Contact your local chamber of commerce for information on how to volunteer to help with parades and other community events.

Call the local chapter of the Red Cross. Sign up for first-aid classes with some of your friends.

Pray for schools and businesses in your community.

Volunteer to help plant trees in local parks. (Talk with the local park service to find out more about volunteer opportunities.)

Adopt as a grandparent a senior at a care facility. Visit your adopted grandparent several times each month.

Age-Old Funds

MATERIALS

○ paper

○ markers

○ optional—blank greeting card

PREPARATION

Contact your church leaders about a giving project your church is currently involved in, or ask church leaders for direction in choosing your own giving project.

PROCEDURE

1. Talk with students about the giving project in which you have chosen to participate.

2. Help students plan ways to earn the same amount of money as their ages (one dollar per year). **What are some chores you can do around your house that your parents might pay you to do? What are some things your neighbors need help with?** (Walking a dog. Baby-sitting. Feeding a pet or collecting newspapers/mail when neighbors are out of town. Yard work.) Distribute paper and markers. Students make lists of ways they can earn money (see sketch). Students decorate their lists. Set a date by which students are to collect money.

3. Students complete tasks at home to earn money and bring money back to class. Students present money to church member in charge of giving project. (Optional: Prepare a card to send with the money to the project you have chosen.)

TEACHING TIPS

1. Determine the best resource to donate to the project (money, clothing, medical supplies, canned food, etc.). If it is something other than money, encourage students to bring the same number of items as their age (a pack of eight pairs of socks or ten large bandages, for example).

2. Encourage students to tell family and neighbors what they are earning money for. If possible, give students brochures on the giving project to show their family and neighbors.

3. If you have siblings in your class, encourage them to work together to earn money.

ENRICHMENT IDEA

Organize a bake sale or other fund-raiser and display signs that encourage people to donate money according to their age. Students use all proceeds for the giving project.

TYLER'S
Moneymakers
• Make Bed
• Take out trash
• Brush and walk Bailey
• Rake leaves
Goal: $10.⁰⁰

Back-to-School Gifts

MATERIALS
○ materials needed for gathering items in the manner in which students decide

PREPARATION
Contact a local school, community center or children's shelter to learn about any children who could not afford school supplies. Make arrangements to deliver items.

PROCEDURE
1. **What are some items that you need for going to school?** (Pencils, pens, pencil sharpeners, backpacks, folders, binders, paper, notebooks, rulers, lunch boxes, erasers, small staplers, etc.) **Some students aren't able to afford these items, so we are going to collect extras of these items for them.** Students vote to decide if they want to bring in items themselves, do a fund-raiser to get money to purchase the items or organize a drive to collect items at church or in their neighborhoods.

2. Depending on the way students have decided to gather the items, students do one of the following: students decide which items they will provide and write postcards to remind themselves to buy extras of that item when they go shopping for school supplies; or students make posters or flyers advertising the fund-raiser (bake sale, candy sale, work day, etc.) or collection time and place, and then put posters or flyers around the church or around their neighborhoods.

3. Students complete collection process and assemble items into kits, putting each set of items into a backpack, shoe box or lunch box.

TEACHING TIPS
1. This project is great to do in the fall, but it would be appreciated by schools anytime during the year.
2. If you are donating items to a school, suggest that a staff member distribute kits secretly so that the recipients are not embarrassed.

OPTION FOR OLDER STUDENTS
Older students may write letters to local businesses, asking them to contribute supplies. Be sure students include information about the project, the recipients and a contact number.

Bag Lunches

MATERIALS

- ⭕ brown bags
- ⭕ plastic sandwich bags or plastic wrap
- ⭕ sandwich ingredients
- ⭕ potato chips
- ⭕ fresh fruit
- ⭕ drink boxes
- ⭕ napkins

PREPARATION

Contact a homeless shelter or soup kitchen to find out how many bag lunches they could distribute for lunch or with the hot meal they serve. Make arrangements to deliver bag lunches.

PROCEDURE

1. **Homeless shelters and soup kitchens normally serve only one or two meals each day. But the people who live in the shelters or go to the soup kitchens get hungry just as often as we do! Let's make some bag lunches to give to people at (name of shelter or soup kitchen), so they will have an extra meal to eat.** Students wash hands before assembling lunches. Students help lay out lunch ingredients in a line on tables.

2. Students form an assembly line to prepare sandwiches, place sandwiches in plastic bags or in plastic wrap, and then place all lunch items in brown bags.

TEACHING TIPS

1. Ask if your church has a budget for buying food to distribute to people in the community. Your church may be willing to donate the money to buy the items for this project.

2. Include coupons from local fast-food restaurants in the lunches. Make sure the restaurants are within walking distance of the shelter or soup kitchen.

OPTION FOR YOUNGER STUDENTS

Students decorate lunch bags before putting items in them.

OPTION FOR OLDER STUDENTS

Students write encouraging notes to put in the lunch bags. Messages might be "God loves you and hears your prayers" or "Someone in (city name) is praying for you." When students are finished packing lunches, lead them in praying for the recipients of the lunches.

ENRICHMENT IDEA

If a church kitchen is available for use, students bake cookies to put in lunches. Students decorate bags and assemble lunches while cookies are baking and cooling.

Boxed Help

MATERIALS

- ○ large sheet of paper
- ○ markers
- ○ large cardboard box
- ○ a variety of decorating materials (construction paper, stickers, etc.)
- ○ postcards
- ○ postage stamps
- ○ pens
- ○ poster board

PREPARATION

Contact a local shelter for people in need and ask for a list of useful items students could donate (clothing [new socks and underwear, new or used clean T-shirts, sweatshirts, sweaters, pants], school supplies [pencils, pens, erasers, notebooks, crayons, folders, scissors], entertainment items [books, board games, puzzles, drawing tablets], etc.). List items on a large sheet of paper. Make arrangements to deliver collected items.

PROCEDURE

1. Begin a month-long project to collect items for a shelter. Talk with students about the items on your list.

2. Divide class into three groups. Students in one group work together to decorate a large box in which to collect items. Another group addresses and writes postcards to students in the class, reminding them to bring items needed. The third group makes a poster listing items to collect and telling when and where to bring items.

3. Display poster on classroom door or in hallway and mail postcards during the week. Collect items in the decorated box. Deliver box at end of project.

OPTION FOR YOUNGER STUDENTS

Students think of toys they have outgrown and could give away or of inexpensive toys they could purchase (jump ropes, balls, frisbees, small cars or action figures, etc.). Students bring toys to put in the box.

OPTION FOR OLDER STUDENTS

Students hold a bake sale to earn money for items they desire to purchase. Students set up a table and sell baked goods after a church service or during a coffee and fellowship time.

ENRICHMENT IDEA

Students make flyers with information about items needed. Photocopy flyers and place them on cars in the church parking lot or post at gathering spots around the church. (Obtain permission from church leaders as needed.) Place the collection box near the main entrance to your church for the next few weeks.

Breakfast in a Bag

MATERIALS

- ○ measuring cups
- ○ quick oatmeal
- ○ powdered milk
- ○ sugar
- ○ raisins
- ○ resealable plastic bags
- ○ plastic spoons
- ○ self-adhesive labels
- ○ markers

PREPARATION

Contact a homeless shelter or soup kitchen to find out how many breakfasts they could distribute. Make arrangements to deliver breakfasts.

PROCEDURE

1. **Homeless shelters and soup kitchens often serve only one or two meals each day. We can show God's love to people who don't have a place to live or enough food to eat by making breakfast bags to give to them.** Students wash their hands.

2. Students place measuring cups, oatmeal, powdered milk, sugar and raisins on tables. Give each student several resealable plastic bags. Each student places 1/3 cup oatmeal, 1/3 cup powdered milk, 1 teaspoon sugar and 12 raisins in each bag. Students place plastic spoons in bags and then seal the bags.

3. On self-adhesive labels, students write "Add one cup hot water, stir and enjoy!" and then place labels on bags.

TEACHING TIP

Ask if your church has a budget for buying food to distribute to people in the community. Your church may be willing to donate the money to buy the items for this project.

OPTION FOR YOUNGER STUDENTS

Print labels ahead of time.

OPTION FOR OLDER STUDENTS

Students assemble Evangelism Booklets (pp. 111-116) and staple one booklet to each breakfast bag.

Canned Food Drive

MATERIALS

○ large sheets of paper or poster board
○ markers
○ tape or tacks

PREPARATION

Contact your church office for the name of an organization which distributes canned food and boxed staples (rice, macaroni and cheese, etc.) to needy people. Contact the organization to learn food items that are most needed. Make arrangements to deliver food items.

PROCEDURE

1. Distribute poster board and markers. Students make posters encouraging others in the church to donate canned food and boxed staples. **What could you draw or write on your poster so that people in our church family will bring donations of food?** Invite students to tell their ideas before they draw pictures and write headlines. Be sure to include the specific kinds of canned food and boxed staples that are needed and the dates on which students and others may bring in canned food and boxed staples.

2. Talk with students about where to display the completed posters. If time allows, students help you put up the posters in those locations.

TEACHING TIP

Ask if your church has a budget for buying food to distribute to people in the community. Your church may be willing to donate the money to buy the items for this project.

OPTION FOR YOUNGER STUDENTS

Students may wrap paper around cardboard boxes and decorate boxes as receptacles for the donations. Place decorated boxes around the church next to each poster.

OPTION FOR OLDER STUDENTS

Students create slogans to put on the signs, such as "Donate Here. Someone's stomach will be glad you did!" Students may also decorate collection boxes with the slogans.

ENRICHMENT IDEA

Arrange for students to volunteer one afternoon after school at a food pantry that distributes food to needy people. Contact parents to form carpools to drive from the schools to the food pantry. Check if it is possible for students to distribute the same food they collected. Before you go, prepare students by talking with them about what they may see and hear.

Celebration Kits

MATERIALS

○ materials needed for the kit type of your choice (see types below).

PREPARATION

Contact a homeless shelter for families, a low-income day-care center or a tutoring center and ask if they would be interested in receiving kits to help children celebrate an upcoming holiday or birthday. Ask how many kits they would like to receive and make arrangements to deliver the kits.

PROCEDURE

1. **What are some of the things you like to make for (Christmas)?** Volunteers respond. **Today we're going to make some kits so that kids who don't have money for food or crayons or paper can make (cards) and (Christmas cookies).** Lead students in assembling one or more types of kits.

2. Deliver kits to the shelter or center at least one week in advance of the celebration.

BIRTHDAY KITS

Students wrap shoe boxes in birthday wrap, wrapping boxes and lids separately. Students fill boxes with balloons, streamers, party hats, noisemakers, party napkins, coupons for ice cream and other treats from local restaurants, individually wrapped candies and small toys.

CHRISTMAS KITS

Students put some of the following items in each Christmas gift bag: sugar cookies in Christmas shapes and tubes of frostings for decorating the cookies, white and colored construction paper, Christmas wrap or tissue paper, blunt-tipped scissors, a glue stick, markers or crayons, envelopes, curling ribbon, a children's book about the first Christmas.

EASTER KITS

Students fill each Easter basket with an egg-dying kit, plastic eggs, stickers, paper, blunt-tipped scissors, tape, crayons (including a white one for eggs), jelly beans, instructions and materials for tissue-paper flowers, and a children's book about the real meaning of Easter.

VALENTINES KITS

Cut two large paper hearts out of red poster board for each kit. Students staple hearts together along the edges and staple a handle across them to create carrying cases (see sketch). Students fill each heart case with construction paper, a glue stick, blunt-tipped scissors, paper doilies, markers or crayons, ribbon, postage stamps, envelopes, tissue paper and conversation heart candy.

TEACHING TIPS

1. The children who will be receiving the kits are often without opportunity to exercise their creativity. Stimulate their imaginations with some of the following extras in each kit: fabric scraps, colorful wallpaper samples, old magazines with colorful pictures, chenille wires, pine cones or dried leaves, clay, stencils, nontoxic paints and brush, brown lunch bags.

2. Send out letters or make phone calls ahead of time to notify students about the project and to encourage them to bring extra supplies from home.

OPTION FOR YOUNGER STUDENTS

Encourage younger students to sort similar supplies into piles and mix together a variety of construction paper colors or markers and crayons. Younger students may each be in charge of one item to put into each kit.

OPTION FOR OLDER STUDENTS

For each kit (and as an example), students make cards with messages wishing the recipients of the kits a great holiday.

ENRICHMENT IDEA

Arrange for some students to deliver the kits to the shelter or center. Bring along the materials for a simple holiday craft for the students to do together with the children at the center. Before you go, prepare students by talking with them about what they may see and hear.

"Change" a Life

MATERIALS

- ○ Change-Box Pattern (p. 75)
- ○ photocopier
- ○ paper
- ○ glue sticks
- ○ card stock
- ○ scissors
- ○ markers
- ○ tape

PREPARATION

Contact your church leaders about a giving project your church is currently involved in, or ask church leaders for direction in choosing your own giving project. Photocopy a Change-Box Pattern for each student, plus one. Practice making your own Change Box with the extra pattern.

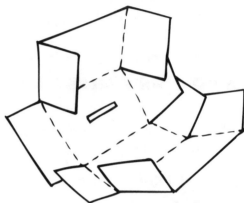

PROCEDURE

1. Explain giving project to students. Give each student a copy of the pattern. Students carefully glue pattern to a sheet of card stock, trimming and lining up all edges. Students decorate one side as a change box.

2. Students cut along solid lines, bending paper in half to cut out the small rectangular shape in the middle. Students then fold along dotted lines and form box by bringing up the edges along the folds, tucking in the side flaps. Students place tape along the joined edges.

3. Each student takes his or her box home and attempts to fill it with coins. Students may also ask others to drop coins in the box and/or do extra chores to earn money to put in the box.

4. Students bring boxes back the following week and open boxes, combining all coins. Students work together to count money collected.

TEACHING TIP

Giving projects could include buying books or games for a local tutoring center or other organization that helps children in need, giving money to an after-school program for sports equipment or buying T-shirts for people in a homeless shelter.

OPTION FOR YOUNGER STUDENTS

Students decorate small boxes with slits cut in the top and tape boxes shut instead of using pattern.

Change-Box Pattern

Christmas in the Summer

MATERIALS

○ large sheet of paper
○ pens
○ wrapping paper
○ marker
○ photocopier
○ tape
○ paper

PREPARATION

Contact a local organization that provides for the needy in your community. Ask about ways to contribute to the organization (money, materials or supplies needed, etc.). Decide on a place where the items can be collected and a time by which they should be collected. Make arrangements to distribute flyers and to deliver collected items.

PROCEDURE

1. Explain to students that you will be having "Christmas in the Summer" for a local organization. Tell students about the needs of the organization.

2. On a large sheet of paper, list name of organization you will be collecting items for, items needed and the date and place items should be brought. Students use information on large sheet of paper to make flyers telling about the project. Photocopy several flyers for each student. Students distribute flyers (place on cars in church parking lot or post in church or neighborhood).

3. After students have collected items, students wrap them to give as presents to the organization. Include small gift tags (made from wrapping paper) on the presents if desired.

TEACHING TIPS

1. Complete this project during the months of June, July or August, when people are not consumed with other giving projects, and students can advertise the "Christmas in the Summer" idea.

2. Contact Samaritan's Purse for information on sending Christmas gifts to needy children around the world or contact Royal Family Kids' Camps, Inc., for information on providing birthday presents for abused children. See pages 147-148 for contact information.

OPTION FOR OLDER STUDENTS

Students make announcements about the project in adult Sunday School classes and hand out extra flyers for the adults to pass on to friends.

Early Morning Entertainment

MATERIALS

- ○ paper
- ○ markers
- ○ cardboard box
- ○ items to fill box (crayons, board games, etc.)

PREPARATION

Contact a homeless shelter for families and ask if they would be interested in receiving items that would keep children occupied in the early morning hours. Find out how many children are at the shelter and whether or not there is a room or separate area in which children can do activities away from the sleeping area. Make arrangements to deliver box.

PROCEDURE

1. **What are some of the things you like to do when you wake up before the rest of your family?** Students respond. **What are some things we could provide for children to do in a homeless shelter before their parents wake up?** (Board games, paper and crayons to color or write letters, instructions for games, books.)

2. Students write a list of activities children in a homeless center could do and what supplies would be needed. Students decorate cardboard box, choose what supplies from the list to bring the following week and write notes to themselves as reminders.

3. Collect items in cardboard box and deliver box to shelter.

TEACHING TIP

Many homeless shelters have a large number of people sleeping in one room. The varied schedules and ages makes getting enough sleep difficult. Providing entertainment for children in early morning hours helps parents and other people at the facility get the sleep they need.

OPTION FOR YOUNGER STUDENTS

Students think of a recent art or craft activity they have done and talk about what materials were needed. Make a list of materials they name and write down the steps they say are necessary to complete the project. Include project items and directions in the box.

OPTION FOR OLDER STUDENTS

Arrange to take your students to the homeless shelter. Call the shelter the day before you go to check the ages and number of children who will be there. Before you go, prepare students by talking with them about what they may see and hear. Take board games or other toys, a morning snack and paper, crayons and markers to entertain the children. If possible, leave the toys and board games at the shelter for future use.

First-Aid Help

MATERIALS

○ resealable plastic bags

○ first aid items (bandages, premoistened cleaning wipes, small bars of soap, individually wrapped aspirin and antacids, etc.)

PREPARATION

Make arrangements to deliver individual first-aid bags to a shelter. Ask the shelter how many bags they could use and if they have any specific recommendations for what to include in the bags.

PROCEDURE

1. Explain the project to students, telling them who will benefit from the project. Students wash hands before assembling bags.

2. Students arrange items for bags in a line, placing plastic bags at the beginning of the line. Form an assembly line by having each student or group of students in charge of one type of item. Students pass each bag down the line or around the table, putting one of their items in the bag before passing it on.

OPTION FOR YOUNGER STUDENTS

Students assemble kits of personal items (toothpaste, toothbrushes, soap, tissues, shampoo, etc.).

OPTION FOR OLDER STUDENTS

Students make small cards to include in the first-aid kits. Messages on the cards could say something about God's love and care.

ENRICHMENT IDEA

Depending on the type of shelter and your locale, students may add survival kit items (plastic garbage bag, energy bars, tablets to make drinking water safe, a whistle, a bandanna, waterproof matches, a moon blanket, etc.) to the first-aid bags and pack them in larger resealable plastic bags.

Meal Add-On

MATERIALS

○ ingredients needed for the meal addition of your choice (see ideas below).

PREPARATION

Contact a local rescue mission or homeless shelter regarding contributing part of a meal they will be serving. Make arrangements to deliver meal items.

PROCEDURE

1. **Rescue missions and homeless shelters care for people who don't have money or a place to stay. We can help by preparing some food that will be part of one of the meals served at (name of mission or shelter).** Students wash their hands. Lead students in preparing one or more of the meal additions that will be served as part of a meal at a rescue mission or homeless shelter.

2. Refrigerate any prepared items until delivered to the mission or shelter for a meal.

TOSSED SALAD

Students wash, dry and cut lettuce, green onions, cucumbers and other vegetables. Students toss lettuce and other vegetables together and place in large resealable plastic bags. Include a bottle or two of salad dressing when you deliver the salad.

JELL-O SALAD

Students cut up fresh or canned fruit on plastic plates. Students prepare Jell-O, following package directions, in a rectangular baking pan and add cut up fruit when Jell-O is partially set.

GARLIC BREAD

Students cut several loaves of French bread in half, spread soft butter along halves, sprinkle garlic powder over butter and wrap loaves in aluminum foil.

TEACHING TIPS

1. Carefully supervise students when they use sharp knives.
2. Send letters to parents ahead of time, inviting them to assist the project by donating needed ingredients.

OPTION FOR YOUNGER STUDENTS

Choose only one of the meal addition ideas. While some students help with food preparation, other students decorate paper place mats with messages about God's love. Deliver the place mats with the meal addition to be used at the shelter.

Meals for a Day

MATERIALS

- ○ Menu Plan page (p. 81)
- ○ photocopier
- ○ paper
- ○ markers
- ○ envelopes
- ○ postage stamps
- ○ box or grocery bag

PREPARATION

Contact your church office for the name of a needy family. Be sure to find out how many people are in the family. Photocopy Menu Plan page. Make arrangements to deliver food items.

PROCEDURE

1. Tell students about the family in your community for whom you will be preparing meals. Students talk together to plan a menu for an entire day's worth of meals for the family. Volunteer fills out Menu Plan page. Each student chooses menu items to bring. Students write letters and address envelopes to themselves as reminders to bring the items needed to assemble meals the following week.

2. Mail the letters early in the week and include for parents a note describing what your class is doing and for how many people.

3. The following week, students write short notes to the needy family, telling about themselves and/or what they like about the meals they planned ("Hi, my name is John. I love to eat spaghetti without breaking any of the noodles. I hope you like it, too."). Students put food items, Menu Plan page and notes in a box or grocery bag.

TEACHING TIPS

1. If students are familiar with the family you are giving meals to, consider keeping the name of the family confidential to avoid embarrassing children in the family.

2. Encourage students to bring the items in containers they are willing to donate to the family or that the family can dispose of. Include paper plates and bowls and plastic utensils.

OPTION FOR YOUNGER STUDENTS

Students decorate brown grocery bags to put the meals in for transporting to the family.

ENRICHMENT IDEA

Plan meals and complete the grocery shopping for an entire week's worth of food for a needy family. Students look through simple recipes and decide on a shopping list, trying to plan meals which use common ingredients. Students bring money for one or more of the meals. Have several students accompany you to do the grocery shopping and deliver the food items.

Menu Plan

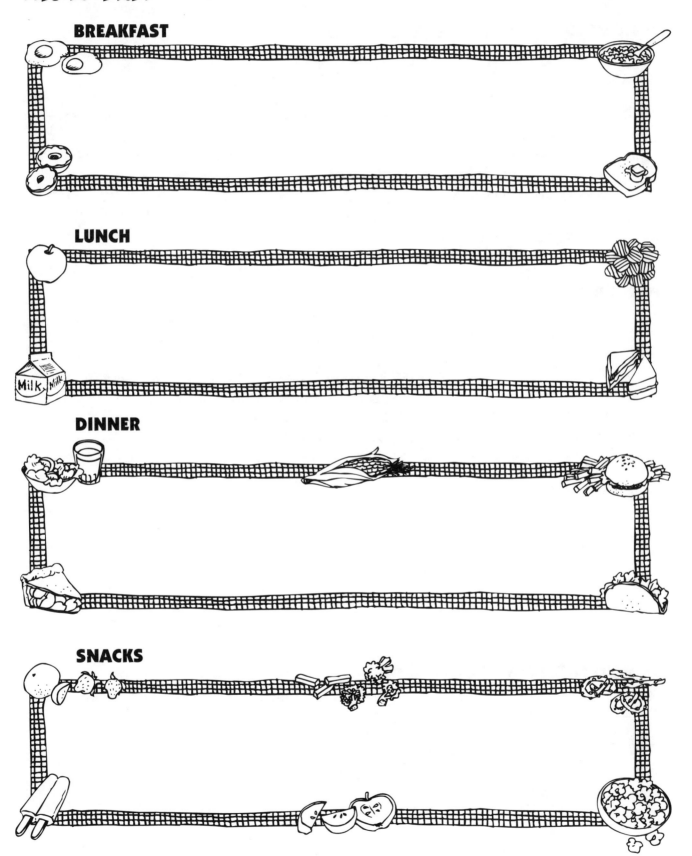

BREAKFAST

LUNCH

DINNER

SNACKS

Party Fun

MATERIALS

○ paper

○ pens

PREPARATION

Contact a local homeless shelter for families or a home for children. Set up a date for a party and ask about any necessary details (size of the room, number of children, shelter rules, etc.) for having your students come to give the party.

PROCEDURE

1. Tell students about the party you have arranged. Prepare students for visiting the shelter or children's home by telling them what they may see and hear. Give students specific guidelines of how to act at the shelter or children's home (stay with the group, look for ways to help, etc.). Discuss what kinds of items (ice cream and cookies, plastic spoons and bowls, napkins, decorations, etc.) and activities (games, singing, etc.) are needed for the party. Students volunteer to bring items and do different tasks such as decorating, serving the food, cleaning up, leading children in a game, etc. Make a list of what each student is responsible for.

2. Students bring items to designated site on the day of the party. Enjoy the party together!

TEACHING TIPS

1. Ask several parents to help with the party. See page 140 for ideas on involving parents.

2. If appropriate, talk to students about the children they will be serving at the party. Give students some examples of subjects that are OK to talk about with the children (how old the child is, the child's favorite interests, what grade in school they are in, etc.) and subjects that would not be appropriate (why the child is in the facility, where the child's parents are, etc.).

OPTION FOR YOUNGER STUDENTS

Students make invitations for the children, inviting them to the party and talking about what will happen there (games, eating ice cream and cookies, etc.).

OPTION FOR OLDER STUDENTS

Students make up several games to play with the children at the party. Students practice games ahead of time to make sure they work well.

Snack Sacks

MATERIALS

○ paper bags

○ items needed to put in the snack bags of your choice (see ideas below).

PREPARATION

Contact a local tutoring center, preschool for low-income children or a homeless shelter and ask if they would be interested in receiving snack bags to distribute. Ask how many bags are needed. Make arrangements to deliver snack bags.

PROCEDURE

Students wash their hands. Lead students in assembling one or more of the types of snack bags described below.

AFTER-SCHOOL SNACK BAGS

Students place juice boxes, granola bars and fruit snacks (or fruit) in brown paper lunch bags. Students may decorate bags before filling them and may include one or more of the following surprise items as well: pencil, stickers, comic book, small rubber ball or jacks.

BEDTIME SNACK BAGS

Students place fruit, cheese and cracker containers and juice boxes in brown paper lunch bags. Students may add items such as toothbrushes and toothpaste, small bars of soap, washcloths and, possibly, small stuffed animals.

OPTION FOR YOUNGER STUDENTS

Students draw pictures or make small cards wishing the recipients a good night's sleep or hoping they had a good day at school. Students put cards or pictures in bags.

OPTION FOR OLDER STUDENTS

Students follow Bookmaking Pattern (pp. 84-85) to make eight-page books from one sheet of paper. Students make a small comic book or bedtime storybook for each of the sacks (talk together with students about what topics would be appropriate for the book) or students write out and illustrate the day's Bible story or main lesson idea.

ENRICHMENT IDEA

Use pillowcases for the bedtime sacks. Purchase pillowcases with kid-friendly patterns or pictures, or have students draw designs with fabric paints or permanent markers on plain pillowcases.

Bookmaking Pattern (side 1)

Cut on the solid black lines and follow the directions to make the book.

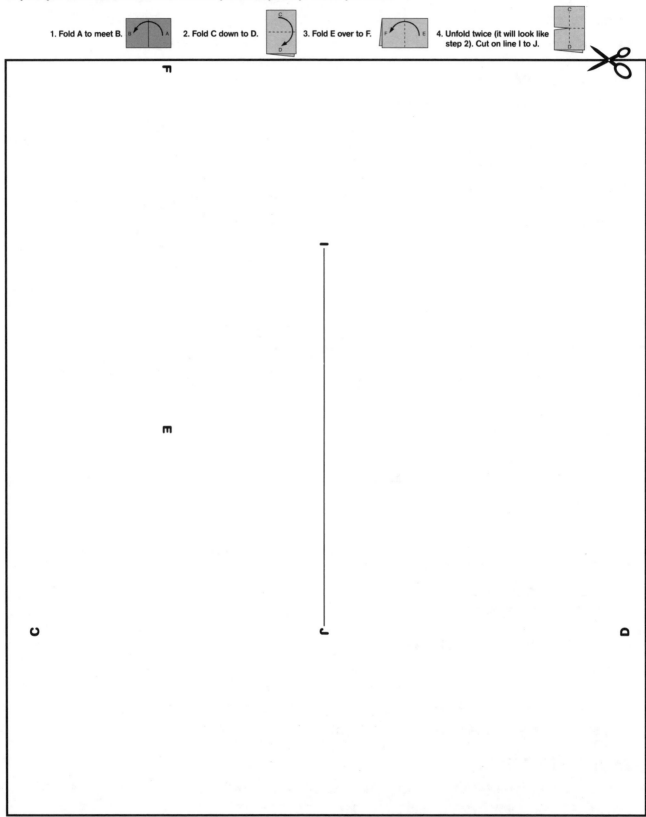

1. Fold A to meet B.

2. Fold C down to D.

3. Fold E over to F.

4. Unfold twice (it will look like step 2). Cut on line I to J.

Bookmaking Pattern (side 2)

5. Open paper completely. Fold G to H.

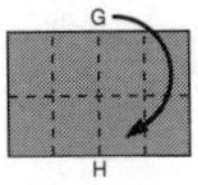

6. Push from ends so that I meets J. Press down on folds to form book.

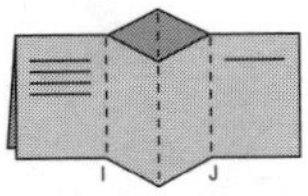

B

H

G

A

Story Time

MATERIALS

- children's storybooks
- audiocassette recorder
- blank audiocassettes
- bell

PREPARATION

Make arrangements to deliver books and tapes to a low-income day-care center or after-school center.

PROCEDURE

1. **Learning how to read helps kids get better grades in school. We can help kids in (name of day-care or after-school center) learn to read by giving them books that we record.** Students look through storybooks and decide on one or two stories to record. Students practice reading the books aloud.

2. Assign each student a page or two of the story to read. Students sit or stand in order of pages being recorded. Ask a volunteer to ring the bell when it is time to turn each page. An additional volunteer begins recording by announcing the title and author of the story and saying, "Turn the page when you hear this bell." Volunteer rings the bell as an example. Students read and record the story.

TEACHING TIPS

1. Instead of a bell, use a whistle or triangle. If none of those are available, a volunteer may say "DING" each time a page should be turned.

2. If you have a large number of students, divide class into several groups. Each group makes a separate story tape. Provide several cassette recorders, blank audiocassettes and storybooks.

3. Encourage students to practice reading the story with a lot of expression and enthusiasm so that the story will sound interesting and lively.

OPTION FOR YOUNGER STUDENTS

Read the story aloud. Students plan sound effects to make as you read the story. Practice reading the story with students' sound effects several times. Then record story and sound effects.

OPTION FOR OLDER STUDENTS

Students decide on a different voice to use for each story character, or each student reads the dialogue of a different character. An additional student may act as the story narrator, reading all the other lines.

Surprise Packages

MATERIALS

- large sheet of paper
- markers
- index cards
- toilet paper tubes (one for each student)
- wrapping paper
- scissors
- tape
- chenille wire
- optional—Evangelism Booklets (pp. 111-116) or other gospel tracts, small gifts (stickers, wrapped candy, gum, etc.)

PREPARATION

Make arrangements to deliver packages to an organization that gives food to needy people, so packages can be distributed along with food items.

PROCEDURE

1. **What do people need to know about Jesus?** (Jesus loves us. Jesus is God's Son. Jesus died on the cross and came back to life again so that we could be forgiven and have eternal life. Jesus is alive.) List students' ideas on large sheet of paper.

2. Give each student an index card, marker and a toilet paper tube. Each student writes one or more sentences about Jesus on an index card. Student rolls or folds the index card and places it in a toilet paper tube. (Optional: Students add Evangelism Booklets or other gospel tracts, and other small gifts to the tubes.) Students wrap tubes with wrapping paper and close ends with chenille wire twists (see sketch).

TEACHING TIPS

1. Bring paper and hole punches for students to make confetti to put in the tubes along with the index cards.

2. If you don't have enough toilet paper tubes, cut apart paper towel tubes or wrapping paper tubes.

OPTION FOR YOUNGER STUDENTS

For a younger class, precut wrapping paper pieces to fit the rolls.

OPTION FOR OLDER STUDENTS

Students visit the organization with you to deliver packages and help distribute packages and food items to needy families. Before you go, prepare students by talking with them about what they may see and hear.

Terrific Toys

MATERIALS

○ materials needed for making the toys of your choice (see descriptions below)

PREPARATION

Contact a local shelter or low-income day-care center to make arrangements to deliver toys students make.

PROCEDURE

1. **Everyone loves toys! (Name of shelter or day-care center) needs some fun toys for children to play with. We can help by making some things for the children to play with.**

2. Lead students in making the toys of your choice.

HOMEMADE BEANBAGS

Students fill clean socks three-fourths of the way full with dried beans. Students tie the top of the sock in a tight knot or have an adult helper stitch the opening shut. (Optional: Students sew two 4-inch [10-cm] squares of fabric together [right sides facing] using needle and thread and leave one side open. Students turn bag right side out and fill with dried beans. Then students sew opening closed.) Store and deliver beanbags in a bucket or a plastic container that can be used in a bean-bag tossing game.

FELT BOARDS

Students work together to cover a few large rectangles of cardboard with felt, securing the felt to the back of the cardboard with masking tape. Other students may cut objects such as geometric shapes, houses, cars, trains, trees, flowers, animals and people out of a variety of types of materials (magazines, wallpaper samples or fabric) and back the objects with felt or strips of sandpaper. (Optional: Provide cardboard patterns of shapes for students to trace around.)

OPTIONS FOR OLDER STUDENTS

1. Older students may enjoy making blocks. Ask a lumberyard to cut a 2x4 or a 2x2 board into small pieces in a variety of shapes (cubes, rectangles, etc.). Students use sandpaper to sand rough corners and edges of the blocks. Blocks may be painted with nontoxic paint before being delivered.

2. Students make sock puppets following the directions and using patterns on pages 101 to 102.

Gift Bags

MATERIALS

○ materials for the type of bags of your choice (see ideas below)

PREPARATION

Contact a tutoring center, local missions organization or immigration services center for recommendations of needed items. (The tutoring center may already supply notebooks and pencils, for example.) Make arrangements to deliver bags.

PROCEDURE

1. **People who come from other countries might not speak English. They may also feel lonely without their families or old friends. What are some other problems they might have?** (They might not understand street signs. They might not have enough money to buy things they need. They might not have any friends nearby.)

2. **Today we are going to help people who have come from another country by making gift bags with some supplies in them.** Students assemble gift bags of your choice for immigrants in your community.

LEARNING BAGS

Give each student a large resealable plastic bag. Students place pencils, erasers, notebooks, rulers, crayons, scissors or other school items in each bag.

SNACK BAGS

Give each student a small paper bag. Students place an individually wrapped snack (cookies, muffin, crackers, raisins, etc.), a box of juice, a fun pencil or other small school item in each bag.

FOOD/HOUSING BAGS

Each student puts several cans or boxes of food in a grocery bag. Students also put bath or dish towels, light bulbs, dish soap and other household items in each bag.

TEACHING TIPS

1. Other ideas for gifts include Bibles or short stories written in English, wallets, backpacks, local maps, dishes, silverware, or gift certificates to a housewares store.

2. Send out letters about the project the week before, asking students, members of an adult Sunday School class or other church group to supply the items for the gift bags.

OPTION FOR OLDER STUDENTS

Students list important places in your community, such as the library, post office, stores, parks, etc. Students write out clear directions to all locations and photocopy one list for each gift bag.

Prayer Magnets

MATERIALS

○ Magnet Borders page (p. 91)
○ photocopier
○ paper
○ poster board
○ ruler
○ pencil
○ scissors
○ markers
○ glue
○ adhesive-backed magnets (available at craft stores)

PREPARATION

Contact a local missions or aid organization to come speak to your students about some of the problems faced by people who have come from another country. Ask your guest to tell about a specific family students can pray for. Photocopy one Magnet Borders page for each student. Cut poster board into 3-inch (7.5-cm) squares, one square for each student.

PROCEDURE

1. Introduce your guest and have him or her speak to the students. Allow time for students to ask questions if the guest is willing.

2. **Praying for people is one way to care for them.** Give each student a Magnet Borders page, scissors and a poster-board square. Students make prayer reminders about the needs of the family described by the guest. Each student cuts out one of the borders on his or her Magnet Borders page and glues border to poster board. Student then writes a slogan or draws a picture inside border. Student then attaches a magnet to the back of the poster-board square. Students make additional magnets as time allows.

3. Conclude the session by having volunteers pray aloud for the family they learned about. Students take magnets home and put in visible places, so they will often be reminded to pray for this family.

OPTION FOR YOUNGER STUDENTS

Ahead of time, print on each poster-board square "Pray for (family your guest is talking about)." Hide the squares around the room before students arrive. When guest is finished speaking, tell students to hunt around the room for a special message. Students find poster-board squares, decorate around the words and attach magnets.

OPTION FOR OLDER STUDENTS

Students make a small prayer journal by folding in half several sheets of white paper and stapling one edge to form a booklet. Students take journals home and write their prayers on the journal pages.

Magnet Borders

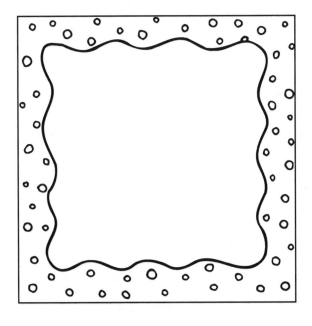

Seasonal Service

MATERIALS

- ○ paper
- ○ pens
- ○ envelopes
- ○ postage stamps
- ○ bags

PREPARATION

Contact a local mission, aid organization or immigration services center to ask about distributing clothes to immigrants. Make arrangements to deliver collected items.

PROCEDURE

1. **What are some of the clothes you need for (winter)?** Volunteers respond. **Some people who have just come to our town from other countries might not have (warm) clothes or the money to buy them.**

2. Distribute paper and pencils. Students write letters to themselves as reminders to sort through their closets with their parents, looking for clothes in good condition they no longer need. Students address envelopes to themselves.

3. Mail letters to students at the beginning of the week. Students bring clothes to your next meeting. Deliver donated clothes to organization you contacted.

TEACHING TIPS

1. Write and photocopy a letter to parents to be included with the students' letters. Encourage the entire family to sort through their closets and, if needed, launder the clothes before donating items.

2. Students may also want to make (to put with the clothes bags) an invitation to your church. Include the name of a person on your greeting committee for the recipient to contact if he or she does attend a service.

OPTION FOR YOUNGER STUDENTS

Write a letter as a class and photocopy letter to mail to each student.

OPTION FOR OLDER STUDENTS

Students sort clothes collected by size and type. Students put clothes of the same size in one bag and label it. Students may also sort the items into types of clothing or shoes.

Baby Bags

MATERIALS

○ grocery bags

○ baby items of your choice (diapers, diaper wipes, rash lotion, baby clothes, receiving or crib blankets, pacifiers, washcloths, hats, crib sheets, baby soap or lotion, bottles, formulas, tissues, a new mother's devotional book, baby books, etc.)

PREPARATION

Talk with a local hospital's maternity ward, a local maternity home, a local social worker or a Visiting Nurses Association to make arrangements to distribute the bags.

PROCEDURE

1. **How many of you have a younger brother or sister? What kinds of things did your brother or sister need when he or she was first born? A new baby needs many things. Some families need help getting all of those things. Today we're going to make gift bags for new mothers who can't afford all the items a baby needs.**

2. Students assemble bags, putting one of each item in the bags.

TEACHING TIPS

1. Instead of using grocery bags, put the items in cloth diapers gathered together with a diaper pin, in small plastic laundry baskets or in diaper bags.

2. Contact local stores and ask them to donate items for the bags, or lead students in a fund-raiser to purchase items.

OPTION FOR YOUNGER STUDENTS

Students bring used toys or books in good condition and include these items in the bags for the baby's older brothers or sisters. Make a note on the outside of the bag stating that the bag is for a baby with siblings.

OPTION FOR OLDER STUDENTS

Older students make invitations to your church to place in the bags. Students should explain on the invitations where the nursery and/or new mother's room are located in the church.

ENRICHMENT IDEA

Make a Second-Step Bag to deliver to families with children over a year old. Include items like baby food, cereals, T-shirts or other clothing items and books and/or toys. Give to a social worker or a doctor's office to distribute.

Cheer Mail

MATERIALS

- ⭕ paper
- ⭕ markers
- ⭕ envelopes
- ⭕ postage stamps

PREPARATION

Obtain the addresses of several hospitals in your area, especially any children's hospitals.

PROCEDURE

1. **When have you been sick for a long time? How did other people help you or encourage you while you were sick? What are some things you could do to encourage someone who is so sick that he or she has to stay in the hospital?** (Tell them funny jokes. Write letters that say you care and want to be friends. Tell them about things you do and say that you wish they were with you. Send pictures.)

2. Distribute materials. Students write letters and draw pictures for children their age who are patients in a hospital. Students address the envelopes to "Patients between the ages of (the ages of your students)" and send letters to a local children's hospital or to the children's ward of a large hospital in your area.

TEACHING TIPS

1. If students need ideas for their letter writing, encourage them to write about their daily activities or interests as though they were writing to their best friends.

2. Use an instant camera to take pictures of students to include in letters.

OPTION FOR YOUNGER STUDENTS

Preaddress envelopes.

OPTIONS FOR OLDER STUDENTS

1. Students make audiocassettes for children in a hospital. Provide blank audiocassettes and a tape recorder. Students tell about themselves, play and sing favorite songs and tell jokes on the tape.

2. Students make cards using the Pop-Up Card Pattern (p. 95). Students use markers to decorate cards and write messages.

ENRICHMENT IDEA

Encourage students to become pen pals with patients. Have students note the request in the letter and include a self-addressed, stamped envelope for a reply. Notify parents ahead of time to obtain any permission needed.

Pop-Up Card Pattern

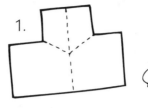 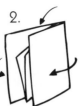 

1. Cut on solid lines.
2. Fold on dotted lines, folding the top section into the card at an angle.
3. Cut a simple shape, such as a heart or flower, into the pop-up piece.

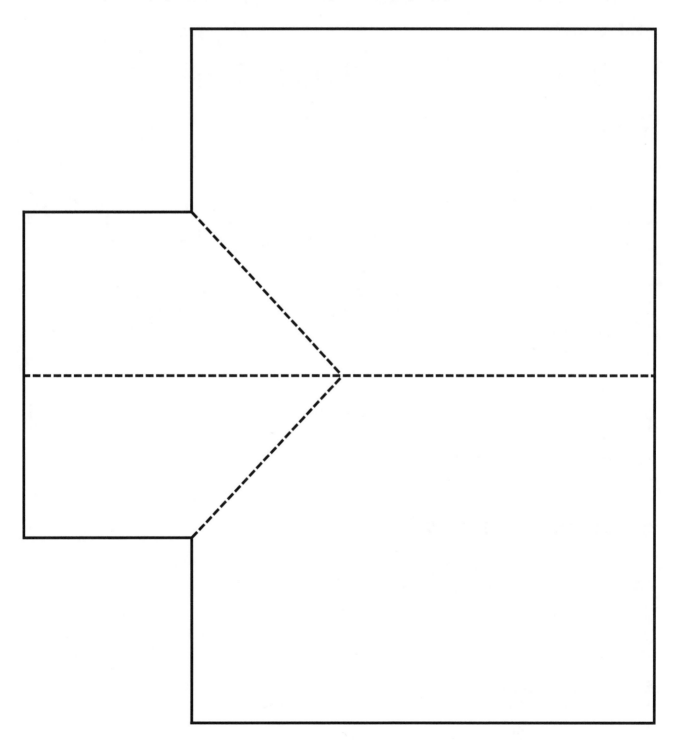

Christmas Caroling

MATERIALS

- ○ paper
- ○ markers
- ○ photocopier
- ○ Christmas carol lyrics from songbook or Internet
- ○ colored construction paper or card stock
- ○ staples and staplers

PREPARATION

Organize an outing to a local senior care facility during the holiday season to sing Christmas carols. Prepare a flyer to give to your students explaining the outing and inviting parents to accompany the students. Photocopy words to five or six familiar Christmas carols (obtain permission for photocopying as needed).

PROCEDURE

1. **Christmas is a great time to visit people and remind them of God's love for them.** Distribute copies of one of the Christmas carols you prepared. **What words or phrases in this song tell about God's love? We are going to prepare for a Christmas caroling party at (name of senior care facility).** Prepare students by talking with them about what they may see and hear at the facility. Give students specific guidelines for how to act at the facility (stay with the group, listen patiently when someone at the facility talks to you, etc.). Distribute flyers you prepared, explaining time and location of caroling outing to students.

2. Students assemble the photocopied carols between sheets of construction paper or card stock to make booklets. Students staple booklets together and decorate covers.

3. Practice singing the carols together.

OPTION FOR YOUNGER STUDENTS

Students bring individually wrapped candy canes to hand out to the residents as carols are sung.

OPTION FOR OLDER STUDENTS

Enlarge song lyrics when you photocopy them. Students illustrate carols, assemble into books and tie pages together with ribbon. Students give the large-print booklets to residents at the senior care facility.

ENRICHMENT IDEA

Carol in several different locations through the holidays: a children's home, a home for disabled people, a shopping mall, etc.

Mail Service

MATERIALS

○ Bibles   ○ markers   ○ postage stamps

○ paper   ○ envelopes

PREPARATION

Before class, obtain names and addresses of residents of a local senior care facility who would like to receive mail.

PROCEDURE

1. **What kind of mail does your family receive? What kind of mail do you get? Why do people like getting mail?** Volunteers answer. Divide class into groups of no more than four. Assign the name of a senior care facility resident to each group of students, repeating names as needed. Distribute materials to each group.

2. Students work together to write a letter to the person they are assigned. Letters should include information about each student in the group such as names, ages, what they are learning in school, activities at church and school, what they enjoy doing, etc. Suggest students include an encouraging Bible verse in their letters (Psalm 18:2 or Isaiah 40:31). Students may also draw pictures or cartoons, write poems, draw decorations, etc.

3. Students place letters and pictures in envelopes. Address envelopes and mail letters. Be sure to include a return address with the name of your class, so residents can write back if they want.

TEACHING TIPS

1. Senior adults often have a hard time reading small print. Encourage students to write large enough for senior adults to read easily.

2. If possible, use an instant camera to take pictures of students to include with the letters.

OPTION FOR YOUNGER STUDENTS

Write a letter together for all the residents at the facility. Students dictate letter and then draw pictures to send with the letter.

OPTION FOR OLDER STUDENTS

Students make a video for residents at the facility. Video can show students singing songs, telling about themselves and/or reading Bible verses.

ENRICHMENT IDEAS

1. Provide small flowering plants to deliver with the letters.

2. Students plan a performance of songs, skits and readings for the senior care facility. Before you go, prepare students by talking with them about what they may see and hear.

Nature Collages

MATERIALS
○ Bibles
○ 12-inch (30-cm) squares of poster board (one for each student)
○ markers
○ glue
○ a variety of nature items (acorns, leaves in a variety of colors and shapes, dried grasses, etc.)

PREPARATION
Contact a local senior care facility to make arrangements to deliver collages students make.

PROCEDURE
1. **Some elderly people are unable to attend church and are in senior care facilities. What would it be like if you were unable to go to fun places?** Volunteers tell opinions.
2. Give each student a square of poster board. Student writes Psalm 136:1 (or other Bible verse) on the poster board and then glues nature items to make a border and decorate the poster board. Students may also use markers to draw seasonal items on the poster board.

TEACHING TIP
Before beginning the activity, have students help you collect nature items on church grounds.

OPTION FOR YOUNGER STUDENTS
Instead of writing messages, students cut out verses from Bible Verse Cards page (p. 54) and glue to poster board.

OPTION FOR OLDER STUDENTS
Students each collect 8 to 12 straight twigs of similar length. Students arrange twigs to make square picture frames and then use hot-glue gun to hold twigs together. Students cut poster board to fit frames and write Bible verses on the poster board. Students glue poster board inside frames and then decorate.

Puppet Fun

MATERIALS

○ Puppetry Guidelines page (p. 100)

○ photocopier

○ paper

○ appliance box or other large piece of cardboard

○ scissors

○ markers

○ puppets

○ children's music cassette/CD and player

PREPARATION

Arrange to perform a puppet show for the residents of a senior care facility. Photocopy Puppetry Guidelines page for each student. Prepare a flyer to give to your students explaining the outing and inviting parents to accompany the students. Cut a large piece of cardboard to stand up as a puppet stage for students to hide behind (see sketch).

PROCEDURE

1. **Everyone needs to laugh and have fun. We can help some people who live at (name a senior care facility) have fun by putting on a puppet show for them.** Prepare students by talking with them about what they may see and hear at the senior care facility. Give students specific guidelines for how to act at the facility (stay with the group, listen patiently, etc.).

2. Students decorate cardboard to look like a curtained stage (see sketch).

3. Give Puppetry Guidelines page and a puppet to each student. Read guidelines together and then have students practice making their puppets move and talk. Play several fun songs. Students choose one or two songs they want to use for their puppet show. Students practice song with puppets.

TEACHING TIPS

1. Arrange a carpool from your regular location if it is too hard for parents to get their children to the senior care facility.

2. Invite someone in your church who works with puppets to give your students some pointers as they practice the song(s).

OPTION FOR YOUNGER STUDENTS

Because younger students' hands are too small to use most ready-made puppets, students make and use Animal Sock Puppets (pp. 101-102).

OPTION FOR OLDER STUDENTS

Students make up a short puppet skit to perform along with song(s).

Puppetry Guidelines

1. Use three or four bounce steps to make your puppet enter and exit the stage.

2. Make sure your puppet is high enough so that it can be seen.

3. Open your puppet's mouth one time for every syllable.

4. Make your puppet look at the audience.

5. Move your puppet so that it looks alive.

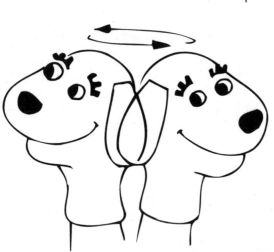

Animal Sock Puppets Instructions

MATERIALS

○ Animal Features Patterns page (p. 102)
○ photocopier
○ paper
○ clean socks

○ 1-inch (2.5-cm) safety pins
○ 3-inch (7.5-cm) rubber bands
○ felt

○ marker
○ glue
○ scissors

PREPARATION

Photocopy Animal Features Patterns page for students to use to while working. Make a sample puppet following the directions below.

PROCEDURE

1. Give each student a sock, safety pin and rubber band. Students turn socks wrong side out and safety-pin rubber bands to toe of socks as shown in sketch a. Students turn socks right side out and insert hands into socks. Rubber bands are slipped over fingers to form mouths of puppets (see sketch b).

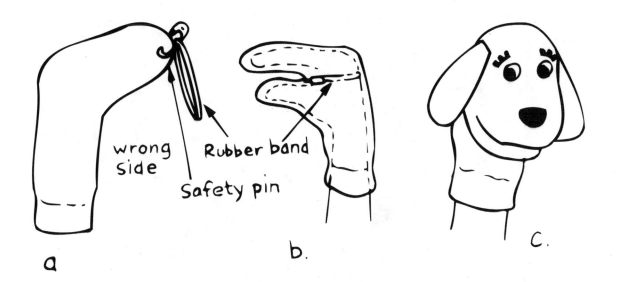

wrong side
Rubber band
Safety pin

a.

b.

c.

2. Students cut ear, mouth and eye patterns they want to use from Animal Features Patterns and then trace them onto felt. Students cut out felt pieces and glue them to socks (see sketch c).

Animal Features Patterns

DOG

CAT

Tray Brighteners

MATERIALS

○ large index cards
○ markers
○ materials for decorating brighteners of your choice (see ideas below)

PREPARATION

Contact a local hospital, meal delivery service or nursing home that could use the brighteners for its residents' or clients' meal trays. Make arrangements to deliver brighteners. Choose the type of brightener that would be most appropriate for the hospital patients, delivery service clients or facility's residents and make a sample.

PROCEDURE

1. Show students the brightener you made. **What kind of people might enjoy seeing something like this on their meal tray?** (People who are sick in a hospital. People who always have to eat their meals in bed.) **Today we're going to make tray brighteners like this for (patients) in (St. Francis Hospital).**

2. Students fold index cards in half to make brighteners.

PICTURE ESCAPES

Students cut nature scenes from magazines and glue them to one side of the index cards. On the other side, students may write "God cares for you!" or some other encouraging message.

SEASONAL GREETINGS

Students decorate index cards for an upcoming holiday, adding heart stickers and a "God loves you!" message for Valentines; fall leaves and a message of thanks for Thanksgiving; etc. (Optional: Students cut up old seasonal greeting cards and attach pictures and/or designs to folded index cards.)

GET WELL WISHES

Students attach (or draw) bandages onto folded index cards and write "Get Well Soon."

OPTION FOR YOUNGER STUDENTS

Talk about some pictures that people might enjoy (animals, nature scene, happy faces, etc.). Students draw pictures on index cards and dictate a message for you to write on the back.

OPTION FOR OLDER STUDENTS

Students write a Bible verse (for example, Psalm 46:1) on the inside of the index cards.

Dexterity Balls

MATERIALS

○ large heavy-duty balloons

○ funnels

○ fine-grained sand or salt

PREPARATION

Contact a local hospital, nursing home, rehabilitation center or home for disabled people to make arrangements to deliver the balls. Make a sample ball following the directions below.

PROCEDURE

1. Show sample you made. **People who have certain handicaps or are in the hospital for long periods of time often struggle to maintain manual dexterity because they don't use their hands for many things. When their hands and forearms become weak, the people become more dependent on others. Providing these balls will help people at (name of hospital, nursing home, rehabilitation center or home for disabled people) maintain or build their muscles.**

2. Students work in pairs to make balls. Distribute materials to each pair. One student in each pair holds the balloon with the funnel in it while the other student pours about ¼ cup of sand or salt into the funnel, filling the deflated balloon to the base of the neck to make a fist-sized ball. Students tie the balloons closed to secure the balls.

OPTION FOR YOUNGER STUDENTS

Students use colored permanent markers to draw happy faces or other fun designs on the balls.

OPTION FOR OLDER STUDENTS

Invite someone who works in physical therapy to talk with your students about exercises that help to build and maintain muscle. Students write some of the suggested exercises on index cards to distribute along with the balls.

ENRICHMENT IDEA

Ask the facility about any other items students could make to help the patients.

Missions and Outreach

Missions and Outreach

Things to Do on Your Own for People Around the World

MATERIALS

- ○ Things You Can Do for People Around the World page (p. 107)
- ○ photocopier
- ○ paper
- ○ index cards
- ○ scissors
- ○ glue
- ○ markers
- ○ hole punch
- ○ ribbon or yarn

PREPARATION

Photocopy Things You Can Do for People Around the World page—one for each student.

PROCEDURE

1. Give each student eight index cards and a copy of the Things You Can Do for People Around the World page. Students cut out ideas and glue each one onto a separate index card. Students use markers to decorate cards. Students punch two holes at the top of each index card and tie cards together with ribbon or yarn (see sketch).

2. Encourage each student to take his or her cards home and choose one idea to do with his or her family.

Pray for your neighbors who don't know about Jesus.

OPTION FOR YOUNGER STUDENTS

Each student chooses one of the ideas from Things You Can for People Around the World page to cut out, glue to index card and decorate. Encourage students to use the idea during the week.

OPTION FOR OLDER STUDENTS

Students suggest additional things they can do to help others around the world. Print students' ideas on a large sheet of paper. Each student chooses two or three additional ideas from large sheet of paper and writes ways on index cards.

ENRICHMENT IDEAS

1. Students keep a card file of ideas for serving others at church (p. 29), in the community (p. 65) and around the world (p. 107).

2. Students read idea cards at a family mealtime and challenge other family members to try one or more of the ideas on the cards. Families work together to see how many of their chosen ideas they can complete in one week.

Things You Can Do for People Around the World

Try some of these ideas on your own!

Choose a country that seems interesting to you. Visit the library or check the Internet to learn all you can about that country.

Pray for one or two people you see on the news or read about in the newspaper.

Talk with your family about supporting a child in another country through Compassion International or World Vision. (Ask your teacher for information about contacting these organizations.)

Invite a friend to come to church with you.

Collect blankets to give to Red Cross for victims of natural disasters around the world.

Learn how to say in another language "Hello," "Jesus loves you" and "My name is _____."

Ask your pastor or missions director for the address of a missionary. Keep in touch with the missionary.

Pray for your neighbors who don't know about Jesus.

Easter Celebration

MATERIALS

- ○ large sheet of paper
- ○ markers
- ○ paper
- ○ photocopier
- ○ envelopes

- ○ postage stamps
- ○ small slips of paper
- ○ plastic Easter eggs
- ○ small wrapped candies or small boxes of raisins

- ○ stickers
- ○ large sheet of butcher paper
- ○ balloons
- ○ streamers
- ○ decorating items with an Easter theme

PREPARATION

Make arrangements to have a community Easter party in a local park or on church grounds. Invite church leaders to join the party and be available to talk with parents of children who come to the party. Obtain address of families in the neighborhood near your church.

PROCEDURE

1. **Easter is a great time to help people learn about Jesus. We are going to have a party for young children in our church's neighborhood so that they can learn about Jesus.**

2. Divide class into three groups. Each group does one of the projects described below to prepare for an Easter party. Then on the day of the party, students hide Easter eggs and help younger children search for eggs.

INVITATIONS

Students make invitations to the party. On a large sheet of paper, print party information including date, time and location of the party. Students copy information onto sheets of paper to make invitations. Photocopy invitations so that there are enough to mail to families in the neighborhood near your church. Students fold invitations, place them in envelopes and address them to people in the neighborhood.

EASTER EGGS

Provide small slips of paper, markers, plastic Easter eggs, small wrapped candies or small boxes of raisins and stickers. **What could you write to tell a younger child something about Jesus that the child would understand?** (Jesus loves you! Jesus is alive!) Students write simple messages about Jesus on slips of paper. Students fill each Easter egg with a slip of paper, sticker and candies or raisins. Make a large number of eggs to be used in an Easter egg hunt.

DECORATIONS

Students make and plan decorations for the party. Students make a large butcher-paper banner to display in the park or on church grounds during the party. Students write "Happy Easter" or other message on banner. Students use markers to decorate banner. Students also plan where they want to place banner, balloons, streamers and other decorating items.

OPTIONS FOR YOUNGER STUDENTS

1. Make invitations ahead of time.
2. Print messages about Jesus on paper and photocopy for each student. Students cut out messages they want to use in eggs.

OPTION FOR OLDER STUDENTS

Students prepare Evangelism Booklets (pp. 111-116). When booklets are assembled, demonstrate how to read booklet with another person and talk about what it means to be a part of God's family. Then divide class into pairs to practice reading and talking about the booklet. Students place booklets in bags with several pieces of Easter candy. Distribute the bags during the Easter party.

Evangelism Booklets

MATERIALS

- ○ Evangelism Booklet pages (pp. 111-116)
- ○ photocopier
- ○ paper
- ○ scissors
- ○ staplers
- ○ markers or crayons

PREPARATION

Make double-sided photocopies of Evangelism Booklet pages, at least one set of pages for each student plus one extra set. Make arrangements to give completed booklets to children's ministry leaders in your church or community. Assemble a sample booklet.

PROCEDURE

1. Show booklet you prepared and invite a volunteer to read it aloud. **What does this booklet tell us about? Why is this message important? We are going to make these booklets so that (names of people to whom you have arranged to give booklets) can use them when they talk with children about Jesus.**

2. Give each student one set of Evangelism Booklet pages and scissors. To assemble booklets, students follow directions on first Evangelism Booklet page. Students use markers or crayons to color booklets.

OPTION FOR YOUNGER STUDENTS

Assemble booklets ahead of time. Students color booklets.

OPTION FOR OLDER STUDENTS

Lead students in praying for people to whom they want to give booklets. Encourage students to mail booklets or deliver them to friends.

Evangelism Booklet

Make double-sided photocopies of pages 111-116. Cut out the pages on the solid black lines and place in order (A-F). Fold page in half so that page A is at the front. Staple pages at the fold line.

You can get to know God better!

God gave us a wonderful book, the Bible, that tells about God and what He wants us to do. A good place to start reading is the Gospel of Mark, one of four books about Jesus.

You can show His love to others!

Other people can learn that God loves them when you are kind and tell what you know about Jesus.

GOD LOVES YOU!

A

Evangelism Booklet

You can talk to God any time!

Talking to God is called praying. You can pray out loud or just with your thoughts. It's great to talk to God when—

- you're angry, sad or worried
- you're happy and glad
- you've done something wrong and are sorry
- you're thankful that He loves and forgives you!

It's even greater to know that God always listens!

SCHOOL BUS

2ABCD3

Please be with me...

1 ## Do you know that the God who made the universe loves you?

He does!

He loves you so much, He wants you to be His child! God's Word, the Bible, says: "God is love." 1 John 4:8

B

Evangelism Booklet

Welcome to God's Family!

I want everyone to know that

on _____ of _____
Month/Day   Year

I, _____
Name

became a child of God by asking Jesus to forgive my sin and to be with me forever.

MEMBER OF GOD'S FAMILY

2

But, do you know that you and I, and all the other people in the world, have done wrong things—

like forgetting God,
and disobeying Him,
and being selfish
and hurting others?

We have.

Evangelism Booklet

Evangelism Booklet

7 Do you know that when you become a part of God's family, God gives you an awesome gift—eternal life?

He does!

This means Jesus will be with you now and forever!

God's Word says: "For God so loved the world that he gave his one and only Son, that whoever believes in him shall not perish but have eternal life." John 3:16

4 So God sent His Son, Jesus, to show how much He loves you. Did you know that Jesus took the punishment for your sin?

He did!

For me?

Jesus died on the cross so that all the wrong things you've done can be forgiven.

God's Word says: "Christ died for our sins." 1 Corinthians 15:3

Evangelism Booklet

Free Drinks!

MATERIALS

- ◯ large sheet of butcher paper
- ◯ markers
- ◯ photocopier
- ◯ paper
- ◯ card table
- ◯ ice chest filled with ice and drink boxes

PREPARATION

Make arrangements to set up a drink stand in a local park or other well-traveled area in your community. (Note: Set up stand in a location that will not take business away from others.)

PROCEDURE

1. **We hear about free offers on television all the time. What do those offers really mean?** (Advertisers want people to buy something from them. Usually you have to buy something in order to get something less valuable for free.) **God's love is different. We don't have to do or buy anything to receive His love. We can help others understand a little about God's love by inviting them to come to church and by giving them something for free.**

2. Students make signs advertising a free-drink stand; signs should include the words "Free drinks! No donations accepted." Students also make flyers telling about the church, including information about church location and times of church services. (Optional: Make flyers announcing a free children's event at your church such as Vacation Bible School, a puppet show or a children's concert.) Photocopy students' signs.

3. Students set up a card table in a well-traveled area in your community. Students tape signs to the table and give out juice boxes and flyers.

TEACHING TIPS

1. Plan to do this project on a hot day.
2. Be sure to have plenty of adult supervision for this project. If you do not have enough help, invite several parents to join you in this project.

OPTION FOR YOUNGER STUDENTS

Prepare flyers ahead of time.

OPTION FOR OLDER STUDENTS

Students make Evangelism Booklets (pp. 111-116) to distribute along with drinks.

ENRICHMENT IDEA

Have a car wash at your church or a nearby gas station. Instead of accepting donations, offer cookies and gospel tracts.

Invitation to Church

MATERIALS

- ○ Invitation page (p. 119)
- ○ white paper
- ○ photocopier
- ○ large sheet of paper
- ○ scissors
- ○ markers

PREPARATION

Make one copy of Invitation page for each student.

PROCEDURE

1. **One way to help someone learn about God is to invite him or her to a church activity where he or she will hear about God.** Tell students about an upcoming activity to which they could invite their friends. List important information about the activity on a large sheet of paper, including date, time and name of the activity.

2. Give each student a copy of the Invitation page. To make invitations, students trim edges of Invitation pages and fold along the dotted lines. Students decorate the outside of the cards and write information from the large sheet of paper on the inside of the invitations. Students sign invitations. Students distribute the invitations to their friends during the week.

OPTION FOR YOUNGER STUDENTS

Print time, place and date on Invitation page before making copies.

OPTION FOR OLDER STUDENTS

Provide a variety of colors of card stock for students to use in making invitations. Students cut paper with decorative-edged scissors and write words in gold or silver ink.

ENRICHMENT IDEAS

1. Students plan and prepare a fun activity to which they can invite their friends. Students plan several favorite games and decide on food to serve. Older students may prepare and perform a skit or puppet show. Plan the activity for a weekend afternoon and send invitations to kids in the neighborhood and to students who have been absent for a while.

2. Students invite friends and neighbors to watch The Story of Jesus for Children (from Campus Crusade for Christ) or another evangelistic video. See pages 147-148 for information on Campus Crusade for Christ and other organizations with evangelistic tools.

Invitation

Please Come!

What _____

When _____

Where _____

Puppet Show

MATERIALS

- ○ appliance box or other large piece of cardboard
- ○ scissors
- ○ markers
- ○ poster board
- ○ children's music cassette/CD and player
- ○ puppets

PREPARATION

Make arrangements to have a puppet show in a local park or on church grounds. Invite church leaders to attend the puppet show and be available to talk with parents and children who come to the show. Cut cardboard to stand up as a puppet stage for students to sit behind (see sketch).

PROCEDURE

1. **Young children love to see puppet shows! We are going to have a puppet show (at the park). We'll invite children and families (at the park) to watch our puppet show and to visit our church.**

2. Divide class into two groups. Students in first group decorate cardboard to look like a curtained stage. Second group of students creates posters advertising the puppet show, making sure to include date, time and location of show.

3. Students choose one or two songs from a children's music cassette/CD to perform with puppets. Students practice using puppets to sing the song(s). Help students hold their puppets, so the puppets can be seen over the puppet stage. Display posters to advertise the puppet show two or three days ahead of the event.

TEACHING TIPS

1. Invite someone in your church who works with puppets to give your students some tips as they practice the song(s).

2. Refer to the Puppetry Guidelines page (p. 100) for tips on how to use puppets.

OPTION FOR YOUNGER STUDENTS

Because younger students' hands are too small to use most ready-made puppets, students make and use Paper-Bag Puppets (pp. 121-122).

OPTION FOR OLDER STUDENTS

Students prepare two or three worship songs and a short skit that tells about your church. Invite one or two students to introduce songs and skit during the show.

Paper-Bag Puppets Instructions

MATERIALS

○ Paper-Bag Puppet Pattern page (p. 122)
○ paper
○ photocopier
○ 9x12-inch (22.5x30-cm) sheets of tan or brown construction paper
○ markers or crayons
○ scissors
○ lunch-size paper bags
○ glue

PREPARATION

Make copies of Paper-Bag Puppet Pattern page, one for each student.

PROCEDURE

1. Students cut out patterns and then trace head, arm and leg patterns onto construction paper. Students cut out pieces and use markers or crayons to draw facial features on head. Students glue head to flap of paper bag (see sketch).

2. To form feet and knees, students fold legs on dashed lines indicated on pattern. Students glue arms to sides of bag and glue legs to lower edge. Students draw clothing details on bag as shown in sketch.

Paper-Bag Puppet Pattern

HEAD PATTERN

Cut here
for boy.

ARM PATTERN
Cut two.

LEG PATTERN
Cut two.

fold

fold

Bread-Dough Napkin Rings

MATERIALS

○ Napkin Rings Patterns page (p. 124)
○ photocopier
○ paper

○ ingredients and utensils to make dough (see Preparation)
○ poster board
○ scissors

○ glue
○ rolling pins
○ plastic knives
○ pencils

○ cookie sheet
○ oven
○ acrylic paint or spray sealer

PREPARATION

Contact your church mission board or other missions organization to ask about projects your class could raise money to support. Photocopy one Napkin Rings Patterns page for every two or three students.

Make the following dough recipe: Sift 2 cups flour, 1 cup cornstarch and 1 cup salt into large bowl. In small bowl, mix 1 teaspoon glycerin and 1 cup water, stirring well. Slowly add wet mixture to dry ingredients, stirring constantly. Knead dough until stiff and smooth—about five minutes. (This recipe makes enough dough for 8 to 12 napkin rings.)

PROCEDURE

1. Explain missions project for which you will be raising money. **Today we will make napkin rings to sell to earn money for our project.**

2. Divide class into groups of two or three. Distribute Napkin Rings Patterns pages. Students glue patterns to poster board and cut out. Give each student a small ball of dough. Students use rolling pins to roll out dough to a ¼-inch (.75-cm) thickness. Then students lay patterns on top of rolled dough and cut out napkin rings by cutting around patterns with plastic knives. Students use tip of pencil to make designs in the dough. Repeat until all dough is used.

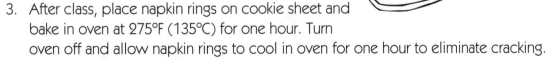

3. After class, place napkin rings on cookie sheet and bake in oven at 275°F (135°C) for one hour. Turn oven off and allow napkin rings to cool in oven for one hour to eliminate cracking.

4. During the next class session, students paint napkin rings with acrylic paint or spray with sealer.

OPTION FOR YOUNGER STUDENTS

Glue patterns to poster board and cut out before class.

Napkin Rings Patterns

Change to Help

MATERIALS

- ○ one baby food jar for each student
- ○ colored tissue paper
- ○ scissors
- ○ liquid starch
- ○ brushes
- ○ 4-inch (10-cm) construction-paper squares
- ○ markers

PREPARATION

Contact an organization that helps needy people to find out ways money given to the organization is used. Ask about projects your class can help raise money to support.

PROCEDURE

1. **Today we are going to make change collectors. During the week, we will use our change collectors to collect spare change from our families and friends. Next week, we will give the money we collected to (organization).** Explain how the organization you have chosen helps needy people and how the money students raise will help.

2. Give each student a jar. Students rip or cut tissue paper into small shapes. Students brush starch on outside of jar and then stick tissue-paper shapes to the starch on the container. Students then brush a layer of starch over the tissue paper on the container.

3. Students fold construction-paper squares in half to make stand-up cards. Students print "Change to Help" on the front of their cards. Encourage students to place jars and cards in a well-traveled place at home or school.

TEACHING TIPS

1. Instead of baby food jars, use margarine tubs or small cardboard boxes. Use craft knife to cut coin slits in the top of each container.

2. Send a letter home to parents explaining how students are to collect money, what the money will be used for and when the jar and money are to be returned.

OPTION FOR YOUNGER STUDENTS

Instead of decorating jars with tissue paper, students use stickers to decorate jars.

ENRICHMENT IDEA

Make a large jar and place it in a well-traveled area of your church. Near the jar, place a sign that tells about your class and why they are collecting money. Ask church leaders to announce your money-raising project to the church.

Kindness Collection

MATERIALS

○ Donation Stationery (p. 127)
○ photocopier
○ paper
○ large sheet of paper
○ marker
○ pens
○ envelopes
○ postage stamps

PREPARATION

Talk with church leaders to determine an appropriate giving project for your students to be involved in. Photocopy Donation Stationery page—at least one for each student. Make arrangements to deliver collected items.

PROCEDURE

1. Explain the giving project and how students can participate. List on large sheet of paper any information students need to know about the giving project (items to be collected for donation, date the items need to be brought to class, instructions to follow, etc.).

2. Distribute stationery, envelopes and pens to students. Each student writes a letter reminding the recipient to participate in the giving project. Students include information listed on large sheet of paper in their letters. Suggest that students also write the reason for the giving project. Each student addresses one envelope to him- or herself. If time permits, some students may write more than one letter to be sent to absentees or to other people the students hope will participate in the giving project.

3. Collect letters and envelopes. During the week, mail the letters to students, making sure each student does not receive his or her own letter.

4. On the appropriate date, collect and deliver items for the giving project.

TEACHING TIPS

1. Instead of having students write individual letters, create a letter with blank spaces for students to fill in with the appropriate information.

2. If students will be collecting used items, ask questions such as, **What could you do to prepare clothing to give away?** (Wash the clothes and fold them neatly.) **Games or books?** (Tape any torn parts.) **Art Supplies?** (Organize them neatly in a decorated box.) Students write ideas in letters.

3. Telephone each student a day or two before the due date to remind them to bring items, or call half your students and ask each one to call one other student.

OPTION FOR YOUNGER STUDENTS

Students find and cut out catalog pictures of items they could collect for the project. Students glue pictures on the back of copies of a short letter you have prepared. Address letters to students and parents and send them out during the week.

Donation Stationery

Rent a Kid

MATERIALS
○ white paper   ○ colored paper
○ pens   ○ photocopier

PREPARATION
Contact a Bible-distribution organization (for example, International Bible Society, Wycliffe Bible Translators or Gideons International) to learn where to send money and where the Bibles will be distributed (see organization list on pp. 147-148). Prepare a flyer as instructed below.

PROCEDURE
1. **There are many people around the world who do not have Bibles. Why do you think having Bibles is important?** (The Bible is God's Word and tells about God's love for us. The Bible tells us the best way to live.) **What are some ways we can earn money to buy Bibles for people who do not have Bibles?** Students tell ideas. Show flyer you prepared. **Doing extra work for neighbors and friends is one way to earn money.**

2. Distribute paper and pens. Students draw pictures and write words on paper to make flyers advertising their willingness to be hired to do housework (washing dishes, dusting, etc.) or yard work (raking leaves, cutting lawn, etc.). Students also tell that money earned will be used to purchase Bibles for people.

HIRE JENNY TO:
☆ walk your dog
☆ feed your pet
☆ sweep floors
☆ rake leaves
☆ bake you a cake
All the dollars earned will be used to buy Bibles for people in Sudan.

3. Photocopy students' flyers on colored paper and provide five copies of each for students to hand out to neighbors and parents' friends. Set a date by which students should complete work and bring money to class.

TEACHING TIPS
Make sure each student gets permission of parent before distributing flyers.

OPTION FOR YOUNGER STUDENTS
Prepare flyers ahead of time. Students fill in information about jobs they are willing to do and then decorate flyers they will hand out.

OPTION FOR OLDER STUDENTS
Students work together to plan a car wash or bake sale. Students make flyers and distribute them several days before the event. Students invite parents and other family members to join them in washing cars or making and selling baked goods.

Woven Straw Wreath

MATERIALS
- raffia
- scissors
- masking tape
- measuring stick
- fishing line
- craft glue

PREPARATION
Contact your church mission board or other missions organization to ask about projects your class could raise money to support. Make arrangements to display and sell wreaths in church lobby or other area. Cut raffia into 3-foot (.9-m) lengths—a handful for each student. Cut fishing line into 6-inch (15-cm) lengths—one for each student.

PROCEDURE
1. Explain missions project you will be raising money for. **Straw decorations are popular in countries all over the world. Today we will be making something like straw wreaths to sell to earn money for our project.**

2. Give each student a handful of raffia. Each student ties ends of raffia together in a knot, leaving a 1-inch (2.5-cm) tail above knot and tapes tail of knot onto hard surface (sketch a). Student separates raffia into three sections and loosely braids sections together until approximately 4 inches (10 cm) are left (sketch b). Student removes tape from braid and holds both ends of braid together to form a heart shape. Student wraps one loose strand several times around the other strands (sketch c).

3. Student glues ends of braid in place, holds ends until dry and trims ends to leave a small fringe. Student ties ends of fishing line to high points on either side of heart (sketch d). The fishing line will help wreath retain its shape and provide a hanger.

OPTION FOR YOUNGER STUDENTS
Braid raffia for students before class.

OPTION FOR OLDER STUDENTS
Students decorate wreaths with dried or silk flowers and ribbons.

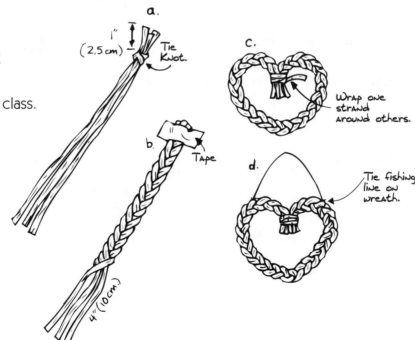

Adopt a Missionary Kid

MATERIALS

○ Missionary Report Form (p. 131)
○ photocopier
○ paper
○ pencils
○ markers

PREPARATION

Ask church leaders for names and addresses of missionaries with children that your church supports. Photocopy and distribute Missionary Report Forms to be filled out by missionary children or people very familiar with the children.

PROCEDURE

1. **Missionary kids live in different places all over the world. They either live with their parents or go to boarding schools. Since they don't get to visit us very often, we can encourage them by writing letters to them.** Divide class into the same number of groups as the number of missionary children about which you have information. Give each group one of the completed forms.

2. Students in each group work together to write a letter and draw pictures for their assigned missionary child. Students tell their names and ages, things they like to do, what they are learning in school, favorite jokes, funny stories, etc. (More than one student can be the same missionary child's pen pal.)

TEACHING TIPS

1. Instead of simply writing letters, students may also make audiocassettes or videotapes to send, or send faxes or e-mail to the missionary children.

2. If students are not familiar with the concept of missionaries, say, **A missionary is someone who tells others the good news about Jesus. Sometimes missionaries live in countries far away from their relatives and home country. Missionary kids need friends who will stay in contact with them, even when they are far away.**

OPTION FOR YOUNGER STUDENTS

Send a letter to just one missionary child. Students work together to dictate a letter. Then students draw pictures of themselves to send to the missionary child.

ENRICHMENT IDEA

Provide a sign-up sheet for students who wish to have additional contact with a missionary kid. This can be elaborate, including sending gifts and cards for birthdays and holidays, or it can be as simple as e-mail messages on the Internet.

Missionary Report Form

From: Name:_____ Age: _____

Birthday: _____ Country: _____ City or region: _____

Language spoken here: _____

How well do you speak the language? (Color in the boxes to tell.)

(Not at all)   (Very well)

Do you have brothers or sisters?

Names:

Ages:

Do you have pets?

Tell us a way your country is different from ours:

What do you usually eat for breakfast?

What do you enjoy most about living in your country?

What do you like least about living in your country?

What's your favorite game? Snack? Book?

What kind of jobs does your family do to tell the people in your country about the good news of Jesus? How do you help?

We'd like to pray for you. What can we pray about?

Encouraging Mail

MATERIALS

- ○ Bibles
- ○ large sheet of paper
- ○ marker
- ○ blank audiocassette
- ○ tape recorder

PREPARATION

Contact your church office or a missions organization to find the names, address and other pertinent information about a missionary family.

PROCEDURE

1. **Today we're going to write and tape-record a letter to a missionary family.** Tell students about the missionary family to whom they will write.

2. Ask questions to help students think of what to write in the letter, printing students' responses on a large sheet of paper. **What might (the Smiths) want to know about our community? Our church? Our class? What is an encouraging Bible verse you would like to tell them? What questions might you ask (the Smiths) about their work? What could you tell (the Smiths) that you will do that might encourage them?** (Pray for them. Tell them a funny story.)

3. Volunteers take turns telling sentences to compose a letter, referring to the ideas on the large sheet of paper. Print letter on a second large sheet of paper.

4. Assign each student one or more sentences of the letter. Tape-record each student reading his or her assigned sentences aloud.

TEACHING TIPS

1. If your class supports someone through a missions organization or is already familiar with a missionary family, write a letter to that person.

2. If students are not familiar with the concept of missionaries say, **A missionary is someone who tells others the good news about Jesus. Sometimes missionaries live in countries far away from their relatives and home country. Missionaries can often get tired because of their hard work. Our letter can help encourage (the Smiths) as they tell people about Jesus.**

OPTION FOR YOUNGER STUDENTS

Students draw pictures of things they like to do and things they have learned about the Bible. Mail the pictures to the missionaries.

Missionary Care Package

MATERIALS
○ Missionary Report Form (p. 131) ○ photocopier ○ materials for package(s) of your choice (see options below)
○ paper

PREPARATION
Ask church leaders for names and addresses of missionaries with children that your church supports. Photocopy and distribute Missionary Report Forms to be filled out by missionary children or people very familiar with the children.

PROCEDURE
Often, missionaries tell other people in countries that are far away about God's great love. Missionaries always enjoy receiving packages from home. Today we are going to work together to make a care package for the (Smith) missionary family. Tell students about the family you have chosen. Then lead students to complete one or more packages to mail to the missionary family.

BIRTHDAY CARDS
Students use construction paper, stickers and markers to make birthday cards for each person in the missionary family. Enclose each person's birthday cards in envelopes labeled "Do not open until (date of person's birthday)." Package all envelopes in one box or mail each of them prior to each person's birthday, allowing ample time for foreign mail service.

COMIC STRIPS
Provide comic strip pages from newspapers. Include as many colored pages as possible. Students cut out their favorite comic strips and glue them onto sheets of paper. Students punch holes in left margin of each sheet and tie together with yarn to make books.

SMALL GIFTS
Students fill a box with stickers, favorite treats (gum, hot chocolate mix, etc.), pencils, crayons, markers, rubber stamps and stamp pad, etc.

TEACHING TIPS
Please keep in mind that missionaries in many countries have to pay high tariffs on items they receive in the mail. Make sure any gifts you send are small and inexpensive. If your class wants to give a more expensive gift, contact your mission board or the missionary's sending agency to find the best way to send your gift.

OPTION FOR YOUNGER STUDENTS
Volunteers tell sentences to write in a group letter to the missionary family. Each student draws a picture to be mailed along with the letter.

Prayer Baskets

MATERIALS

○ Prayer Basket Pattern (p. 135)
○ photocopier
○ colored paper
○ glue sticks
○ scissors
○ slips of paper
○ markers

PREPARATION

Ask church leaders for prayer requests from missionaries your church supports. Photocopy the pattern onto colored paper—at least one for each student.

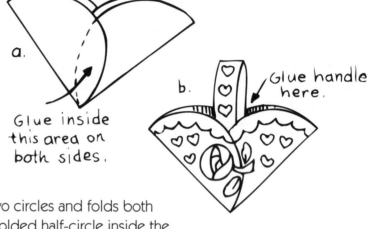

Glue inside this area on both sides.

Glue handle here.

PROCEDURE

1. **We can make baskets to hold papers with prayer requests for our missionaries.** Give each student a photocopied Prayer Basket Pattern. To make basket, student cuts out the two circles and folds both circles in half. Then student slides one folded half-circle inside the other so that the folds meet in a point at the bottom (sketch a). Student then glues inner half to outer half.

2. To make handle, student cuts a strip of paper and glues each end to each inner side of the basket (sketch b). Tell students about prayer requests from missionaries your church supports. Students write prayer requests for missionaries on slips of paper and put requests in baskets. Encourage students to take baskets home and pray about one of the requests each day.

TEACHING TIPS

1. Students decorate outsides of baskets by attaching small stickers or drawing with glitter pens. Rick rack, lace or other trims may also be added.

2. If students are not familiar with the concept of missionaries say, **A missionary is someone who tells others the good news about Jesus. Sometimes missionaries live in countries far away from their homes and families.**

OPTION FOR YOUNGER STUDENTS

Print prayer requests for missionaries on a sheet of white paper. Photocopy one paper for each student. Students cut out prayer requests to place in their baskets.

OPTION FOR OLDER STUDENTS

Students write letters to the missionaries for whom they are praying.

Prayer Basket Pattern

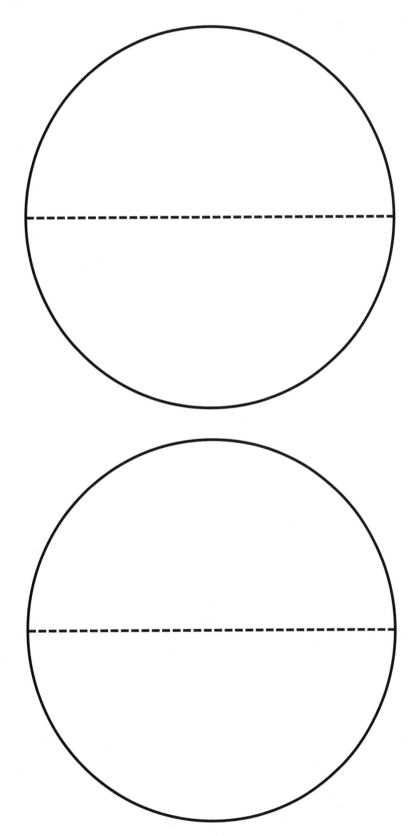

Appendixes

Introducing Service Projects

Bible Basics

Service projects can be great fun! Your students will come to love helping others in practical ways, but students need to understand the reasons for serving others. Here are some Bible passages and questions to help you lead a discussion with your students about why we serve others and how God can use the good things we do to help others learn about Him.

The first time you talk with students about doing service projects, choose one of the following Bible passages to discuss with students. The questions below the Bible passages will guide your students to discover for themselves what the Bible really ly says about loving and caring for others. Continue to use these Bible passages and questions as you work on service projects.

"Of all the commandments, which is the most important?"

"The most important one," answered Jesus, "is this: 'Hear, O Israel, the Lord our God, the Lord is one. Love the Lord your God with all your heart and with all your soul and with all your mind and with all your strength.' The second is this: 'Love your neighbor as yourself.' There is no commandment greater than these." Mark 12:28-31

After reading these verses together, ask the following questions:

- **Why do you think Jesus said these two commandments were the greatest ones of all?**
- **Where are your neighbors? Next door to you? On your block?**
- **Who else might be your "neighbor"?** (Anyone who is in need.)
- **How does this passage say to treat other people?**
- **What are some ways you show love to yourself?**
- **How do you like people to treat you?**
- **When can you treat other people in ways you like to be treated?**
- **What are some things you think might happen if we treated other people the way we like to be treated?**

Love must be sincere. Hate what is evil; cling to what is good. Be devoted to one another in brotherly love. Honor one another above yourselves. Romans 12:9,10

After reading these verses together, ask the following questions:

- **What does "devoted" mean? What do you think it means to "be devoted to one another in brotherly love"?**
- **What ways do you show the people in this room you care about them?**
- **In what ways do you like for other people to show honor and respect to you? How can you show that same honor and respect to others?**
- **What changes might happen in this group if we do what these verses say? What changes might happen in our church? Our neighborhoods?**

Each man should give what he has decided in his heart to give, not reluctantly or under compulsion, for God loves a cheerful giver. 2 Corinthians 9:7

After reading this verse together, ask the following questions:

- **Why do you think people give money and time to God? What do you think is in it for them?**
- **What kind of givers does the verse say God loves? What kinds of giving really make Him happy?**
- **Other than money and possessions, what are some things a kid your age can give to God? What do you think God would give in return?**

Let us not become weary in doing good, for at the proper time we will reap a harvest if we do not give up. Therefore, as we have opportunity, let us do good to all people, especially to those who belong to the family of believers. Galatians 6:9,10

After reading these verses together, ask the following questions:

- **What do you think might be some of the results of showing God's love to people in our church? Through the project we're doing? In our community?**
- **Why do you think Paul told these people not to give up?**
- **What are some opportunities we have to do good? What do these verses tell us to do when we have an opportunity to do good?**

Involving the Family

Kids need to learn a lifestyle of loving and serving others every day. But how can you help them? The best way is to involve their entire families! Lifestyle learning is reinforced in a powerful way when a child sees his or her parent gladly involved in serving others.

Communicate!

Whenever you start a new service project, send home a letter that describes the project, the people who will benefit from it and what steps your group will be taking to help them.

As part of your planning, think of ways you can use the help of parents or other family members. Be sure your letter includes this information and invites parents and other family members to help in the ways described in the letter.

Involve!

Adults and older siblings can

- pray for the project,
- donate needed items,
- approach businesses for donations,
- volunteer to drive,
- chaperone,
- help with administrative details, phone calls and paperwork, and
- help lead small groups.

Younger siblings should not be left out. (They are the next members of your group!) Occasionally schedule an activity or club meeting in which younger siblings are included. Do a project with the younger siblings, using the Option for Younger Students provided for most projects. And consider a service project that benefits younger siblings and their friends, such as Easter Egg Hunt (p. 108-109), Play Dough Fun (p. 40) or Outside-In Party (p. 39)

Expand!

To give families more ideas of ways to serve others, photocopy and send home the Things You Can Do page found in each section of this book (pp. 13, 29, 65, 107). Include a letter to parents, suggesting ways for them to become involved in projects; use sample letter on page 141 as a guide.

Sample Parent Letter

Dear Parents,

Join the adventure at Club Serve! Club Serve is for fourth, fifth and sixth graders with a desire to help others. Students will learn about loving and serving God as they take part in a variety of projects that will benefit people in our church and in our community. We will meet every Tuesday evening from 6:30 to 8:00 in room 204 beginning on September 14.

Our first project will be sending care packages to missionary families from our church. Please join us for a special kick-off event on September 10 at 6:00 in the evening. We will learn about our missionaries and have snacks and games from the countries in which they serve. It will be fun for the whole family!

Please read and fill out the information and permission sheet attached. Return it with your child or, better yet, bring the sheet when you come to our kick-off meeting!

With the prayer support and enthusiastic help of adults in our church, we believe Club Serve will be a place where our kids will be helped to learn a life of hands-on service and where God's love is shared with others! Thank you for participating—and look for good things to come!

In God's service,

Janis Coultrup
555-9292
janis@domain.ext

Medical and Liability Release Form

IMPORTANT: This is a sample form, not intended to be reproduced. A lawyer familiar with the church liability laws in your state should evaluate the form you use.

Church name: _____

Address: _____

Phone number: _____

Child's name: _____

Birthdate: _____ Grade: _____

Address: _____

City: _____ Zip: _____

Phone: _____

Date(s) of activity: _____

Authorization of Consent for Treatment of Minor

I, the undersigned parent or guardian of _____, a minor, do hereby authorize any duly authorized employee, volunteer or other representative of the (church name), as agent(s) for the undersigned, to consent to any X-ray examination, anesthetic, medical or surgical diagnosis or treatment, and hospital care which is deemed advisable by, and is to be rendered under the general or specific supervision of, any licensed physician and surgeon, whether such diagnosis or treatment is rendered at the office of said physician and surgeon or at a clinic, hospital or other medical facility.

It is understood that this authorization is given in advance of any specific diagnosis, treatment or hospital care being required but is given to provide authority and power on the part of our aforesaid agent(s) to give specific consent to any and all such diagnosis treatment or hospital care which the aforementioned physician in the exercise of his or her best judgment may deem advisable.

This authorization shall remain effective from _____ to _____ .

I, the undersigned, on behalf of myself and _____ (child's name), shall indemnify, hold free and harmless, assume liability for and defend the (church name), its agents, servants, employees, officers and directors from any and all costs and expenses, including but not limited to attorneys' fees, reasonable investigative and discovery costs, court costs and all other sums, which the (church name), its agents, servants, employees, officers and directors may pay or become obligated to pay on account of any, all and every demand for, claim or assertion or liability, or any claim or action founded therein, arising or alleged to have arisen out of _____ (child's name)'s use of real or personal property belonging to the (church name), its agents, servants, employees, officers and directors, or by reason of _____ (child's name)'s participation in any (church name) activity(ies).

Parent or legal guardian signature: _____ Date: _____

Home phone: _____ Work phone: _____

Other emergency contact: _____ Phone: _____

Family doctor: _____

Phone: _____

Insurance company: _____ Policy number: _____

Medication/allergies: _____

Last tetanus immunization: _____

Will you allow blood transfusions? _____

Any special needs? _____

Starting a Service Club

Want to turn your older elementary students into lifetime service people? Start a service club! Unlike sports clubs or other performance-related activities, all that is needed to be a member of a service club is a willing heart and hands! It's a great way to involve and include kids who might feel left out of other activities. In addition, a service club provides a setting where showing kindness, compassion and acceptance are the norm, not the exception. Besides all the benefits to the kids and to the community, it's just plain fun! Your club might meet after school, one evening a week, every day during school vacation or only once each month for a special project.

Organization

- Recruit and screen helpers so that you will have at least one adult for every eight to ten children. (Be sure to invite additional adults whenever you go somewhere away from your normal meeting place.)

- Talk with church leaders to determine the best projects for students to work on. Choose projects based on needs, resources and time available; and be sure your projects are more than busy work. Kids will quickly drop out if they sense that their projects don't have real value.

- Several weeks before the club's first meeting, send letters to parents (p. 141) and include announcements in your church bulletin or newsletter (see sample below).

Attention 4th, 5th and 6th graders!

NEW CLUB FORMING NOW!

Club Serve

**Tuesdays from 6:30-8:00 P.M.
beginning September 14 in room 204.**

Join us as we work on interesting activities and fun projects to serve God, help our church and make a difference in our community and in our world!

Call Janis at 555-9292 for more information
or to sign up **NOW!**

- Make most projects short-term, lasting not more than a session or two to complete. Kids tend to lose interest in long-running projects.

Meetings

- Begin each meeting with a short Bible study (see pages 138-139 for Bible passages and discussion questions related to serving others).

- Lead students to pray for each other and also for the people they will be serving. Use a variety of creative prayer methods and consider keeping a club prayer journal.

- Plan for enough time to prepare service projects: kids will have a greater sense of accomplishment if most projects can be completed during the time available. Be ready with materials at hand and have a plan in mind for how best to complete the project. To cut down on direction-giving and to build relationships, you may wish to pair younger children with older ones.

- Plan often to end club time with a fun group game, a snack or other activity that promotes interaction and fellowship.

Enrichment

- Allow time for kids to explore and brainstorm project ideas based on their understanding of needs around them.

- For special projects that might last a period of weeks, invite a volunteer to make a chart or poster on which to record your progress.

- Invite to a club meeting someone from the group that will benefit from the project you're starting. Write a few open-ended questions on cards for club members to use in interviewing this person and learning about needs to be met.

- Make record keeping important! Have someone take notes and another person take photos of or videotape every project. At the end of the year, you'll be ready for a review party. Read notes and look at photos or videotape(s). Kids will be excited to recall how they have served God and made a difference!

Serving with Puppets

One great way to introduce students to serving others is to put on a puppet show for younger children in your church or community. Students of any age can use puppets to tell others about Jesus or teach other important lessons. When teaching students to use puppets, there are several things to remember.

First, choose puppets that are the right size for students. Make sure that students can easily move puppets' mouths. Commercially made rod-arm style puppets vary in size, but normally they can be used by larger fourth- and fifth-grade students. These puppets can be heavy, so be sure that any puppet show you do is short. Younger and smaller students can use smaller commercially made puppets or puppets made following the patterns and directions on pages 101-102 or pages 121-122.

Next, choose songs that are appropriate for your audience. New puppeteers will find short familiar songs easiest to perform. If doing a show for young children, make sure songs are short (one to three minutes) and are easy to understand. Avoid songs that use a great deal of symbolism since young children are literal thinkers.

Teach students to use puppets as tools, not as toys to play with. Actions of puppets can be funny and attention grabbing. Because of this, make sure that actions and fun help to tell the story, not distract from it. Simple guidelines for using puppets are described on page 100. Practice the puppet show several times before performing so that students will feel comfortable during the show.

Service Organizations

Many organizations have needs your students can help fill! For local organizations, first check with your own church officers to connect with programs with which your church may already be involved. Because these organizations are already in contact with your church and your church has a good idea of their needs, one of these organizations might be a good first project choice.

Then use the telephone book and local newspaper as sources. Local rest homes, hospitals, relief agencies, food banks, senior meal programs, youth organizations, homeless shelters, single parents' support groups and local park agencies are all organizations often seeking help! The current needs of the organizations may also be listed in the newspaper from time to time. A phone call to these organizations or their auxiliaries will put you on the track of local needs to be filled. Also don't forget adult service clubs or even the reports you hear on the television news as possible sources of project information.

There are also national and international organizations that appreciate volunteer help or donations. Some of these organizations are listed on pages 147-148. If you are able to explore on the Internet, you can often get immediate information about current needs of these organizations. Naturally, if you want to do an international project, remember that your church's own missionaries are often the perfect connection to people in need in another part of the world!

And, of course, involve your students in your search! Once your students become "service scouts," they will likely come up with a myriad of needs they have noticed—needs that they can help to meet!

Before you plan any service project, contact the organization you want to help. Make sure that your students will be meeting an actual need. Let the organization know how much your students will be able to do and make arrangements to deliver your project to the appropriate place and/or people. Use the Contact Form on page 149 to record important information.

List of Organizations

AMERICAN RED CROSS
PUBLIC INQUIRY OFFICE
431 18th Street NW
Washington, DC 20006
(202) 639-3520
For donations:
(800) HELP-NOW
www.redcross.org

COMPASSION INTERNATIONAL
Colorado Springs, CO 80997
(800) 336-7676
www.compassion.net

CAMPUS CRUSADE FOR CHRIST
NEW LIFE RESOURCES
101 TDK Boulevard, Suite B
Peachtree City, GA 30269
(800) 827-2788
www.campuscrusade.com
For information on the JESUS Video Project:
(800) 295-3787

DOCTORS WITHOUT BORDERS
6 East 39th Street, 8th Floor
New York, NY 10016
(212) 679-6800
www.dwb.org

FEED THE CHILDREN
333 North Meridian Avenue
Oklahoma City, OK 73107-6568
(800) 627-4556
www.feedthechildren.org

FOOD FOR THE HUNGRY
P.O. Box 12349
Scottsdale, AZ 85267
(800) 2-HUNGER
www.fh.org

THE GIDEONS INTERNATIONAL
P.O. Box 140800
Nashville, TN 37214-0800
(615) 883-8533
www.gideons.org

GOODWILL INDUSTRIES INTERNATIONAL
9200 Rockville Pike
Bethesda, MD 20814
www.goodwill.org

INTERNATIONAL BIBLE SOCIETY
1820 Jet Stream Drive
Colorado Springs, CO 80921
(719) 488-9200
www.IBS.org

ROYAL FAMILY KIDS' CAMPS, INC.

1068 Salinas Avenue

Costa Mesa, CA 92626

(949) 548-6828

www.RFKC.org

THE SALVATION ARMY

P.O. Box 269

Alexandria, VA 22313

(703) 684-5500

www.salvationarmy.org

SAMARITAN'S PURSE

P.O. Box 3000

Boone, NC 28607

(828) 262-1980

www.samaritan.org

WORLD VISION

Mail stop 207

P.O. Box 9716

Federal Way, WA 98063-9716

(888) 511-6598

www.worldvision.org

WYCLIFFE BIBLE TRANSLATORS

P.O. Box 628200

Orlando, FL 32862-8200

(800) 992-5433

www.wycliffe.org

Contact Form

Name of organization: _____

Address: _____

_____

Contact person: _____

Best time to call: _____

Phone numbers: _____

E-mail address: _____

Needs of the organization (items needed, jobs to be done, etc.):

_____

_____

RESTRICTIONS

Age: _____

Health: _____

Size of group: _____

Other: _____

Project that best fits needs: _____ Page _____

Delivery/meeting arrangements:

_____

_____

Clip Art

Mark Your Calendar

MARK YOUR CALENDAR

MARK YOUR CALENDAR!

Kids in Action

Kids in Action

Kids in Action

Listen Up!

Listen Up!

Listen Up!

Good News

GOOD NEWS

GOOD NEWS

Good News

Help Wanted

Help Wanted

HELP WANTED

Help Wanted

HELP WANTED

Friends and Family

Church Family

Missions and Outreach

Community

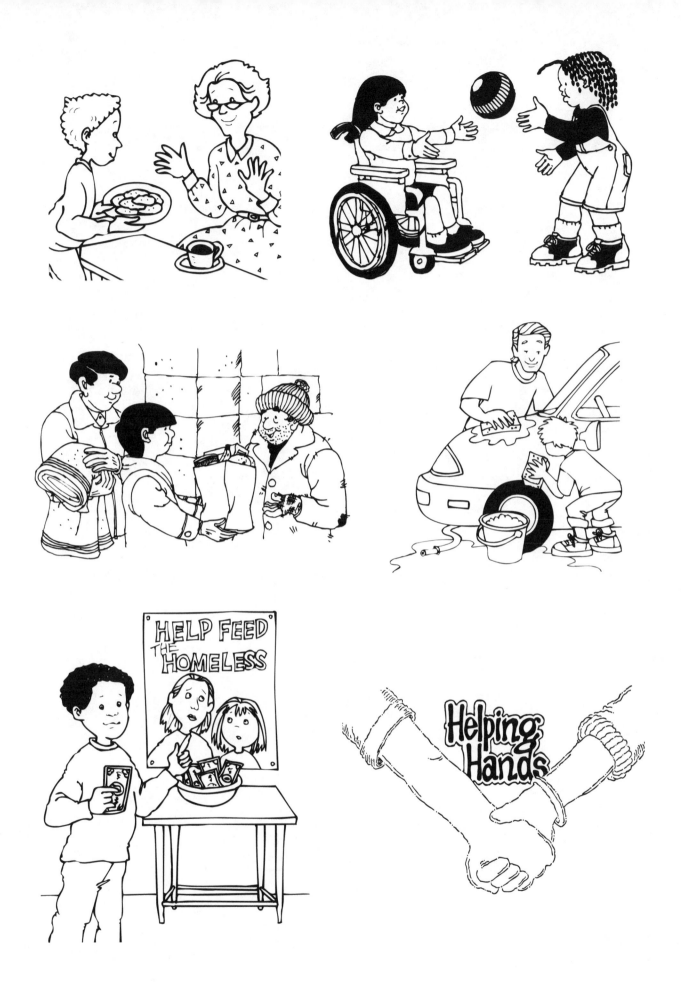

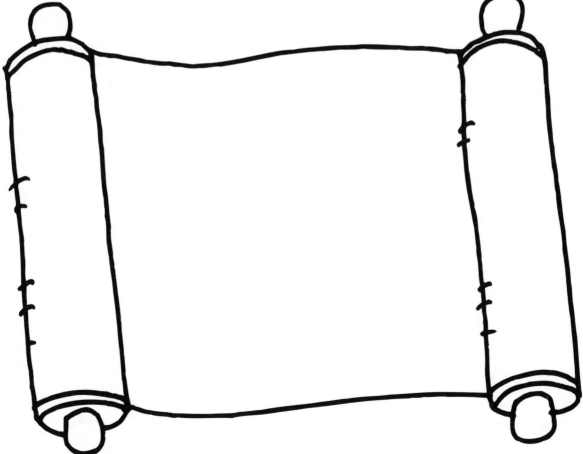

Index

Patterns and Miscellaneous Pages

Projects

INDEX